THE POWER OF A PRAYING LIFE

UNLOCKING MIRACLES THROUGH EVERYDAY PRAYER

By

Frank J. Donohue

Not-Y, Virginia Beach

This is a really great inspirational book for the times we are facing. The Power of a Praying Life *invites you into a deeper, more authentic relationship with God through the power of everyday prayer. Frank J. Donohue shows how prayer can bring peace, clarity, and transformation—no matter where you are on your journey.* **This isn't just a book—it's a lifestyle of prayer.** *I'm going to read this more than once and give it / recommend it for the people I care about.*

—John James, #1 Best Selling Reader

Dedication

I dedicate this book to Francis John, Jared Joseph and to all humans in need of prayer.

PREFACE

Unlocking Miracles Through Everyday Prayer

The three great pillars of Christian living are **almsgiving**, **fasting**, and **prayer**. Initially, I set out to write a few short reflections on prayer during Lent—a simple exercise that could satisfy all three. Write a few pages, check the box, and move on.

But God had other plans.

What started as a small Lenten project turned into a divine assignment. I could feel it deep in my heart and echoing in my mind:
"I want you to use your talents and write a book on prayer to help others."

And so, I listened. I sat down, opened my heart, and began writing—this time, not just as a task to complete, but as a calling to fulfill.

For years, prayer was a mystery to me.

I saw it more as a religious duty than a sacred dialogue. I had my prayer checklist—my wish list of things I wanted God to fix— but if I'm honest, I wasn't even sure He was listening. Prayer felt like talking to the ceiling... tossing words into the wind and hoping something would stick.

But then something changed.

I found myself in a season of deep uncertainty. I didn't have the answers. I didn't even know what to ask for. So, I did the only thing I could: I dropped the formal words and simply cried out, **"God, I need You. I don't know what to do."**

And something shifted—not in my circumstances, but inside me. I didn't hear a loud voice from heaven. There wasn't an immediate miracle. But I felt peace... and for the first time in a long time, I knew I wasn't alone.

That moment taught me something powerful:
Prayer isn't about saying the right words—it's about building a real connection.

As a pilot, I've spent over three decades flying jet airplanes around the world. So, it's only natural that aviation metaphors have found their way into this book.

Up in the sky, I was trained to maintain full control: monitor every gauge, anticipate every storm, follow every flight plan to precision.
I wanted control over everything—just like when I was in the cockpit of my jet. Altitude, heading, turbulence, fuel flow— I thrived on structure, order, and predictability.

But life doesn't work like that.

There's no autopilot for grief. No instrument panel to measure broken relationships. No checklist to fix a weary soul.

When everything around me started to fall apart—my career, my finances, my relationships—I hit a breaking point. I realized that although I had been praying, I was still gripping the yoke of my life too tightly.
I wasn't asking God to lead—I was asking Him to bless my plan.

One night, exhausted and out of options, I finally let go.
"God," I prayed, "I'm done trying to force this. I give it all to You. Lead me wherever You want me to go."

And then something remarkable happened.

The very next day, I got a call—an opportunity I never saw coming. It was better than anything I had planned for myself. And from that day forward, I began to see doors open that I could never have orchestrated on my own. The more I surrendered, the more God led me. The more I trusted, the more peace I found.

Prayer changed everything.

That's why this book was born—not to teach you how to pray *more*, but to help you pray *deeper*.

Not to give you a script, but to invite you into an authentic, powerful, two-way relationship with God.

You don't have to be a spiritual expert or a biblical scholar to connect with God in prayer. You just have to be willing to come honestly, consistently, and with an open heart.

This book is designed to help you do exactly that.

We'll walk through real-life stories, scriptural moments from Jesus' prayer life, and practical tools to help you develop a meaningful rhythm of prayer. At the end of each chapter, you'll find:

✔ **A guided prayer** — to help you apply what you've learned and speak directly from your heart.

✔ **A reflection question** — to draw you deeper into God's presence.

✔ **A real-life testimony** — stories that show how prayer changes lives.

Whether you're just starting your prayer journey or you've been praying for decades, *The Power of a Praying Life* will help you cultivate a prayer life that brings **peace in chaos**, **hope in darkness**, and **power in everyday life**.

So, if you've ever felt like your prayers are weak… if you've struggled to stay consistent… if you're longing to feel connected to God in a real and personal way…

You're in the right place.

This is your invitation.
Let's discover together the incredible, life-changing power of a praying life.

Are you ready to let go—and let God take the lead?
Let's begin.

CONTENTS

Preface..i

Introduction..1

Chapter One: When Words Aren't Enough—Why We Need Prayer...5

Chapter Two: Talking to God Like a Friend—Breaking Free from 'Perfect' Prayers...9

Chapter Three: The Secret Place: Cultivating a Life of Deep, Daily Prayer...13

Chapter Four: Finding Peace in Chaos—How Prayer Can Silence Fear...19

Chapter Five: The Three-Minute Prayer That Can Change Your Day..23

Chapter Six: Letting Go & Letting God—Prayers of Surrender..27

Chapter Seven: Praying Through the Pain—Turning Wounds into Worship..31

Chapter Eight: From Hate to Love—The Prayer That Changes Everything...35

Chapter Nine: Praying for Your Family—A Legacy of Faith...39

Chapter Ten: Prayer and Fasting: Supercharging Your Spiritual Power...45

Chapter Eleven: Hearing God's Voice—How to Recognize His Guidance in Prayer...49

Chapter Twelve: Praying Boldly—Asking for More Without Fear...53

Chapter Thirteen: The Prayer That Moves Mountains— Unlocking Miracles Through Prayer...........................57

Chapter Fourteen: Timeless Paths of Prayer: Prophets, Religions, and Their Spiritual Wisdom................................63

Chapter Fifteen: Walking with Mary: Embracing Deeper Prayer through Her Help and Intercession......................67

Chapter Sixteen: The Power of the Rosary: A Prayer that Echoes Through the Ages..71

Chapter Seventeen: Novenas: The Strength of Nine Days of Intentional Prayer...75

Chapter Eighteen: The Universal Prayer: A Call to Deeper Connection with God.................................79

Chapter Nineteen: Scripture and Prayer: Finding Prayer's Power in the New Testament.................................85

Chapter Twenty: Living a Life of Prayer—Turning Every Moment into a Sacred Conversion.....................91

Chapter Twenty-One: A Prayer Life That Lasts—Making Prayer a Daily Habit..95

Chapter Twenty-Two: Living a Life of Love—How Prayer Transforms Who We Are..............................99

Chapter Twenty-Three: The Secret to a Powerful Prayer Life—Never Stop Praying.....................................103

Final Words: This Is Just the Beginning............107

Conclusion: Your Journey Starts Now..............109

Acknowledgements......................................110

Bibliography..111

About the Author...113

Author's Note..114

INTRODUCTION

Why Prayer Matters

Let me be honest—there was a time when I wrestled with prayer. Not just a little discomfort or confusion, but deep, lingering questions. I didn't always know what to say. I wondered if I was doing it *"right."* And more often than I care to admit, I silently questioned whether God was even listening.

If you've ever felt the same way, you're not alone.

Maybe you've tried praying, but it felt awkward or empty. Maybe life has thrown you curveballs, and your heart is tired, bruised, and wondering if God really hears. Maybe you've prayed for years, but your prayers have started to feel more like routine than relationship. Or maybe you've just never been sure where to start.

I get it. I've been there. But something changed—and it didn't come from mastering a technique or memorizing the perfect words.

It happened on an ordinary night, during an extraordinary moment of weakness. I was overwhelmed. The weight of life was pressing down hard—too many problems, too few answers. So, I did something simple: I stopped trying to impress God. I stopped worrying about the "right way" to pray. And I just talked to Him —like a friend.

No polished words. No holy-sounding phrases. Just raw, honest conversation.

And that night, something shifted. My problems didn't magically disappear—but peace showed up. The kind of peace that whispers, *"You're not in this alone."* That moment changed everything. I realized prayer isn't about performance—it's about presence. It's about connection. It's about inviting God into every corner of your life, not just the polished parts, but the messy, broken, and uncertain ones too.

Prayer isn't a spiritual talent reserved for the super-religious. It's a lifeline for every single one of us.

1

And that's what this book is all about—helping you rediscover prayer not as a duty, but as a relationship. Not as a formula, but as a foundation. Not as a last resort, but as your first and strongest response to life's highs and lows.

This book is here to help you find your rhythm, your voice, and your confidence in prayer. Because no matter who you are or where you are on your journey, God is ready to meet you—and speak with you—right where you are.

Whether you've been praying for years or you're just beginning, *The Power of a Praying Life* will show you how to:

✔ **Talk to God anytime, anywhere—even when you don't have the words.**
✔ **Pray in a way that feels natural, honest, and deeply personal.**
✔ **Trust God in the middle of chaos, confusion, or pain.**
✔ **See real transformation—not just in your circumstances, but in your heart.**

At the end of each chapter, you'll find a short-guided **prayer**, a **reflection question**, and a **simple action step**—practical tools to help you turn what you've read into something you live.

So don't skip ahead. Don't rush past this moment.
Because right here, right now—**God is inviting you into something deeper.**

Are you ready to experience the power of a praying life?
Let's get started.

Section 1
UNDERSTANDING THE HEART OF PRAYER

Laying the Foundation

1

When Words Aren't Enough—Why We Need Prayer

Discovering why prayer is essential to a life of faith.

I used to believe that prayer had to be perfect.

I thought I needed to say the right words, use the right phrases, and sound like I had everything together. But when life got hard —when my heart was heavy and my mind was spinning—I found that my rehearsed prayers didn't work.

Have you ever felt that way?

Maybe you've prayed, but it felt like no one was listening.
Maybe you've wanted to pray, but you didn't know what to say.
Maybe you've even wondered, *Does prayer really change anything?*

If that's you, you're not alone.

Even the disciples—Jesus' closest friends—watched Him perform miracles, calm storms, and raise the dead. But out of all the things they saw Him do, the one thing they asked Him to teach them was:

"Lord, teach us to pray." — *Luke 11:1*

Why?

Because they knew that prayer was the foundation of everything Jesus did. If Jesus—who was God in the flesh—needed prayer, how much more do we?

Prayer Is Not About Getting the Words Right

One of the biggest lies we believe about prayer is that we have to pray the "right way."

But when Jesus prayed, He didn't use fancy words or long, religious speeches. He prayed with honesty, intimacy, and confidence.

When He was in anguish, He cried out:

"Father, if You are willing, take this cup from Me." — *Luke 22:42*

When He was grateful, He simply said:

"Father, I thank You." — *John 11:41*

When He was in pain, He prayed:

"My God, My God, why have You forsaken Me?" — *Matthew 27:46*

Jesus prayed with raw emotion. And that's exactly what He invites us to do.

God is not waiting for polished words—He's waiting for honest hearts.

What Happens When We Pray?

Jesus didn't just pray because it was a habit—He prayed because **prayer changes things.**

When we pray:

✔ **We draw closer to God.** Prayer deepens our relationship with Him.

✔ **We gain peace.** Prayer shifts our focus from worry to trust.

✔ **We invite God's power into our lives.** Prayer opens the door for miracles.

Prayer is not about changing God's mind—it's about aligning our hearts with His.

Guided Prayer

Take a moment to pray, using Jesus' example:

"Father, I come to You just as I am. I don't need to have the perfect words— I just need You. Draw me closer to You. Help me to pray with honesty, just as Jesus did. I open my heart to You now. Amen."

Reflection Question

➡ **What is one area of your life where you need to invite God in through prayer?**

Testimony: How Prayer Brought Peace in the Middle of Chaos

Maggie was a mother of three who felt like her life was falling apart. Her husband had lost his job, their bills were piling up, and she was overwhelmed.

"I was so stressed, I couldn't even pray," she said. "I felt like I had to figure everything out on my own."

One night, completely exhausted, she whispered, *"God, I can't do this anymore. Please help me."*

That was it. No long prayer. No perfect words. Just an honest cry for help.

The next day, she got an unexpected call—an old friend had heard about their situation and offered financial support. Then, a job opportunity opened up for her husband.

"It wasn't about the money or the job," she said. "It was about realizing that God had been there all along. I just needed to turn to Him."

Prayer doesn't have to be complicated. It just has to be real.

2

Talking to God Like a Friend—Breaking Free from 'Perfect' Prayers

How to speak with God openly and honestly.

I used to think I had to pray a certain way for God to hear me. I believed I needed the right words, the right posture, and the right amount of faith for my prayers to "work." But the more I studied the way Jesus prayed, the more I realized:

Prayer is not about performance. It's about relationship.

Think about your best friend. When you talk to them, do you rehearse your words? Do you worry about sounding polished? No—you just speak honestly because you know they care.

That's exactly how Jesus approached prayer.

He didn't use complicated language. He didn't follow a strict formula. He simply talked to His Father.
And that's what God invites us to do too.

Jesus Prayed with Honesty, Not Perfection

In the Garden of Gethsemane, Jesus was facing the hardest moment of His life. He knew He was about to be betrayed, arrested, and crucified. Instead of saying a well-crafted prayer, He poured out His raw emotions:

"Father, if You are willing, take this cup from Me; yet not My will, but Yours be done." — Luke 22:42

Jesus didn't hide His pain.
He didn't pretend to be okay.
He simply told the Father exactly how He felt.

9

If Jesus, the Son of God, could pray with that kind of honesty, why do we feel like we need to have everything figured out before we come to God?

The truth is, God doesn't want perfect prayers. He wants real prayers.

What If I Don't Know What to Say?

Many people struggle with prayer because they don't know where to start. If that's you, here's some good news:

God isn't waiting for the perfect words—He's waiting for you.

If you're hurting, tell Him.
If you're grateful, thank Him.
If you're angry, be honest about it.

In Romans 8:26, the Bible tells us:

"The Spirit helps us in our weakness. We do not know what we ought to pray for, but the Spirit Himself intercedes for us through wordless groans."

Even when we don't have the words, **God knows our hearts.**

Practical Steps: How to Pray Like Jesus Did

If you want to pray more freely, try this simple practice:

1. **Start with "Father."**
   Jesus always began His prayers with *Father* because prayer is about relationship, not religion.

2. **Be honest.**
   Tell God exactly how you feel—whether you're joyful, worried, or struggling.

3. **Listen as well as speak.**
Prayer is not just about talking to God; it's about hearing from Him too.

4. **Keep it simple.**
Jesus' most powerful prayers were short and direct —*"Father, I thank You,"* or *"Not My will, but Yours be done."*

Guided Prayer

"Father, I come to You just as I am. I don't have the perfect words, but I know You hear me. Help me to pray with honesty, the way Jesus did. I don't want to perform—I just want to be with You. Thank You for loving me. Amen."

Reflection Question

➡ **What's one thing you've been afraid to say to God in prayer? Can you bring it to Him today?**

Testimony: How Honest Prayer Changed My Life

David had always felt distant from God.

He grew up in church, but prayer felt like a chore, not a conversation. He memorized prayers, recited words, and checked the boxes. But deep down, he wondered:

"Does God actually hear me?"

One day, during a season of depression, he decided to do something different. Instead of praying a polished prayer, he spoke from the heart:

"God, I don't know what to say. I just feel lost."

For the first time, he felt connected to God—not because of the words he used, but because he finally prayed with honesty.

From that moment on, prayer became a conversation, not a ritual.

11

"I realized that God didn't need me to sound holy. He just wanted me to be real."

3

The Secret Place—Cultivating a Life of Deep, Daily Prayer

Creating space for consistent, intimate time with God.

There is a difference between praying occasionally and living a life of prayer.

Many of us pray when we need something—when life gets hard, when a crisis hits, or when we don't know what else to do. And while God welcomes every prayer, Jesus invites us to something deeper—a daily, consistent, intimate relationship with the Father.

This is what He called **"the secret place."**

Jesus' Example: Prayer in the Secret Place

Jesus didn't just pray in public. He didn't just pray in emergencies. He made private prayer a priority.

"But when you pray, go into your room, close the door and pray to your Father, who is unseen. Then your Father, who sees what is done in secret, will reward you." — *Matthew 6:6*

Jesus didn't say, *"If you pray."*
He said, *"When you pray."*

That means prayer isn't supposed to be an occasional event—it's supposed to be a **way of life**.

He modeled this in His own life:

✔ *Mark 1:35* — *"Very early in the morning, while it was still dark, Jesus got up, left the house and went off to a solitary place, where He prayed."*
✔ *Luke 5:16* — *"Jesus often withdrew to lonely places and prayed."*
✔ *Matthew 14:23* — *"After He had dismissed them, He went up on a mountainside by Himself to pray."*

If Jesus, the Son of God, needed alone time with the Father, **how much more do we?**

What Happens in the Secret Place?

The secret place is where we:

✔ **Develop a deeper connection with God.**
(*James 4:8* – "Draw near to God, and He will draw near to you.")

✔ **Find strength and renewal.**
(*Isaiah 40:31* – "Those who wait on the Lord will renew their strength.")

✔**Receive clarity and guidance.**
(*Psalm 32:8* – "I will instruct you and teach you in the way you should go.")

Prayer is not just about asking for things—it's about spending time in God's presence.

How to Build a Secret Place of Prayer

If you want to develop a strong, consistent prayer life, start here:

1. **Find a Time.**
   Jesus prayed early in the morning—but find a time that works best for you.

2. **Find a Place.**
   It doesn't have to be a physical "prayer room"—it can be a quiet corner, a walk outside, or even your car.

3. **Make It a Habit.**
   Start small. Five minutes a day can grow into a powerful prayer life.

4. **Talk to God, Then Listen.**
   Prayer is not just about speaking—it's also about hearing from God.

14

Guided Prayer: Entering the Secret Place

"Father, I want to know You more. Help me to set aside time each day to meet with You. Teach me to listen, to wait in Your presence, and to grow in my prayer life. I want to dwell in the secret place with You. Amen."

Reflection Question

➡ **What is one step you can take today to create a consistent time of prayer?**

Testimony: How Daily Prayer Changed My Life

Sarah had always struggled with prayer. She believed in God, but she didn't have a daily connection with Him.

"I would pray when I needed something, but I never had a habit of just spending time with God."

One day, she decided to set aside ten minutes each morning. At first, it felt awkward. But over time, something changed.

"I stopped seeing prayer as a duty and started seeing it as a relationship. The more I prayed, the more I felt God's presence—not just in my prayer time, but throughout my whole day."

Now, prayer is her foundation.

"I don't just pray when I need something—I pray because I don't want to go a day without talking to my Father."

Section 2

Praying Through Life's Struggles and Victories

Learning to Rely on Prayer in Every Season.

4

Finding Peace in Chaos—How Prayer Can Silence Fear

Trusting God when life feels out of control.

Anxiety. Worry. Fear.
No one is immune to them.

There are moments when life feels out of control—when uncertainty clouds our thoughts, when fear grips our hearts, and when no amount of reasoning can silence the inner storm.

In those moments, we have two choices:

1. **Let fear take over.**

2. **Turn to God in prayer.**

Jesus knew this struggle. He experienced exhaustion, uncertainty, and pressure beyond what we can imagine. But instead of letting fear control Him, He turned to prayer.

And because of that, He found peace in the middle of chaos.

Jesus Prayed in His Most Overwhelming Moments

One of the most powerful examples of Jesus praying through fear happened in the **Garden of Gethsemane.**

The cross was waiting for Him. The weight of the world's sin was about to be placed on His shoulders. He knew what was coming —pain, betrayal, suffering, and separation from the Father.

And He felt the full weight of it:

"My soul is overwhelmed with sorrow to the point of death." — *Matthew 26:38.*

19

Jesus was not emotionless in this moment. He was deeply troubled, to the point of sweating drops of blood (*Luke 22:44*). But what did He do? **He prayed.**

"Father, if You are willing, take this cup from Me; yet not My will, but Yours be done." — *Luke 22:42.*

Jesus' circumstances didn't change immediately. The suffering didn't disappear. But through prayer, He found peace and strength to face what was ahead.

Prayer doesn't always remove the storm, but it brings God's peace in the middle of it.

How Prayer Calms Fear

Fear thrives in uncertainty. It grows when we focus on what might happen instead of who God is.

That's why prayer is the antidote to fear—it shifts our focus from our problems to **God's power**.

Here's what happens when we pray:

✔ **Prayer reminds us that we are not alone.** (*Isaiah 41:10*)
✔ **Prayer shifts our focus from worry to trust.** (*Philippians 4:6–7*)
✔ **Prayer invites God's presence into our fears.** (*Psalm 34:4*)

Fear fades when we focus on the One who is greater than our fears.

Practical Steps: Praying Through Anxiety

Next time fear threatens to overwhelm you, try this:

1. **Pause and take a deep breath.**

2. **Speak honestly to God about what you're feeling.**

3. **Declare His promises over your situation.**

Example Prayer:

"Father, I feel overwhelmed. Fear is trying to take over my heart. But I know You are bigger than my fears. You are my refuge, my strength, and my peace. I give this situation to You. Help me to trust You instead of worrying. In Jesus' name, Amen."

Reflection Question

➡ **What fear do you need to surrender to God today?**

Testimony: How Prayer Brought Peace in a Time of Crisis

Frank was a father of two when he heard a scream that shook him to his core—the kind of scream no one ever wants to hear.

It wasn't a phone call. It was his wife, crying out in a voice so chilling, so full of terror, it sounded like she'd seen a ghost—or something far worse. "**Francis!**" she screamed.

Frank spun around and looked down the hallway—just in time to see her collapse, face-first to the ground. In an instant, the world tilted. He ran to her side, heart pounding, panic flooding his chest. She was unconscious. Her eyes were closed. And then… she stopped breathing.

In those next 20 to 30 seconds, something primal kicked in. Frank knelt down, grabbed her hand, and began resuscitation—desperate, determined, and pleading with everything he had:

"Breathe! Breathe! Don't you stop breathing!"

Miraculously, even though her eyes remained closed, she gasped —then another breath, and another. His voice, his love, his hands —they brought her back long enough for the paramedics to arrive.

The ambulance crew rushed in, performed a series of checks, and whisked her away to the hospital in a blur of flashing lights and sirens. A **CAT scan revealed the terrifying truth: a ruptured brain aneurysm.** The doctors immediately began assembling an emergency surgical team.

A ruptured brain aneurysm is a life-threatening medical crisis—it happens when a weakened blood vessel in the brain suddenly bursts, causing bleeding into the space around the brain. It's like a balloon popping inside your head—and the damage can be catastrophic. The bleeding increases pressure in the skull, starves the brain of oxygen, and without rapid treatment, it can lead to permanent brain damage... or death.

As the surgery began, Frank sat alone in a hospital waiting room, gripped by fear. His mind was spinning:

What if she doesn't survive?
What if our lives change forever?
I'm too young to lose my wife... My kids are too young to lose their mother.

The hours that followed were a blur of worry and prayer—but in that moment, one thing was certain: life had changed. Forever.

In that moment, he did the only thing he knew to do—**he prayed.**

"God, I don't know what's going to happen, but I know You are with me. I trust You. Please give me peace."

He didn't feel instant relief, but as he sat in that waiting room, he felt God's presence. The fear didn't consume him. Instead, he found the strength to breathe, trust, and hold onto faith.

His wife survived. The recovery was long, but through it all, prayer became her anchor. Of all the death experiences Frank had encountered, it was this moment—watching his wife close her eyes and stop breathing—that stunned him into truly appreciating the power of prayer.

"I used to think prayer was about getting answers," she said. *"But now I realize it's about getting peace."*

5
The Three-Minute Prayer That Can Change Your Day

Simple but powerful ways to invite God into everyday moments.

Many people struggle with prayer because they think it has to be long and complicated.

They believe they need 30 minutes in silence, the perfect words, or deep theological insight to pray effectively.

But Jesus never said prayer had to be long—He said it had to be sincere.

Some of the most powerful prayers in the Bible were short:

✔ *"Lord, save me!"* — Peter, as he sank into the water (*Matthew 14:30*)
✔ *"God, have mercy on me, a sinner."* — The tax collector (*Luke 18:13*)
✔ *"Father, forgive them."* — Jesus on the cross (*Luke 23:34*)

God isn't concerned with how long we pray—**He cares about our hearts.**

That's why even a **three-minute prayer** can transform your entire day.

Why Short Prayers Are Powerful

✔ **They help you stay connected to God all day.** (*1 Thessalonians 5:17*)
✔**They keep prayer simple and approachable.** (*Matthew 6:7*)
✔**They shift your focus from problems to God's presence.** (*Isaiah 26:3*)

When you invite God into your day—even for just three minutes —it changes how you think, how you act, and how you feel.

The Three-Minute Prayer Formula

If you don't know where to start, here's a simple three-step structure for a quick but powerful prayer:

1. Minute One: Praise & Gratitude

- Start by acknowledging who God is and thanking Him.

"Father, thank You for this new day. Thank You for Your love, Your grace, and the breath in my lungs."

2. Minute Two: Surrender & Request

- Release your worries and plans to God.

"Lord, I give You this day. Guide my thoughts, my words, and my actions. Help me to trust You and walk in Your will."

3. Minute Three: Protection & Strength

- Ask God for strength, wisdom, and protection for the day ahead.

"Holy Spirit, lead me. Keep me from temptation, fill me with Your peace, and help me love others well today."

That's it.

Three minutes. One prayer. A changed day.

Ways to Use the Three-Minute Prayer

✔ **In the morning** — Before checking your phone, say it first thing.

✔ **Before work or school** — Invite God into your responsibilities.

✔ **In stressful moments** — Stop, breathe, and pray.

✔ **Before bed** — Reflect on the day and surrender it to God.

The more you pray these short, intentional prayers, the more you'll find yourself talking to God naturally throughout the day.

Guided Three-Minute Prayer

"Father, thank You for this moment of life. Thank You for this breath of air. Thank You for providing water and food for my body, and thank You for protecting, guiding, and nourishing my soul. Please protect and guide my thoughts, words, heart, and soul. Help me to love You, myself and everyone around me. In Jesus' name, Amen."

Reflection Question

➡ **How can you make time for a simple three-minute prayer today?**

Testimony: How a Simple Prayer Changed My Day

Emma used to rush through her mornings—waking up late, grabbing coffee, and jumping straight into work.

"I always felt anxious, rushed, and disconnected from God."

Then she started praying for just three minutes every morning.

"It felt so small at first. But over time, I noticed a huge difference—I started my day with peace instead of stress. I felt God's presence throughout the day. And now, I can't imagine not praying before I start my morning."

Prayer doesn't have to be long to be powerful.
Even a three-minute prayer can change your entire day.

6

Letting Go & Letting God—Prayers of Surrender

Releasing control and trusting in God's plan.

We love control.

We love knowing what's coming next, having a plan, and making sure things turn out the way we expect. But life rarely works that way.

No matter how much we try to hold everything together, there comes a moment when we realize:

✔ We don't have all the answers.
✔ We can't fix everything on our own.
✔ We need God to step in.

This is where **surrender** comes in.

Surrender is not giving up—it's giving over. It's choosing to place our worries, our plans, and our desires into God's hands, trusting that He knows what's best.

But how do we actually do that?

Jesus showed us how.

Jesus' Ultimate Prayer of Surrender

One of the most powerful prayers in the Bible wasn't about asking for something big—it was about letting go.

In the Garden of Gethsemane, Jesus was facing His greatest trial. He knew He was about to be arrested, beaten, and crucified. He knew the weight of the world's sin was about to be placed on His shoulders.

And in that moment, He prayed one of the most difficult prayers of surrender ever recorded:

"Father, if You are willing, take this cup from Me; yet not My will, but Yours be done." — *Luke 22:42*

Jesus was fully God, but He was also fully human. He felt fear, pain, and sorrow. He asked God if there was another way—but He ultimately surrendered to the Father's will.

That's what surrender looks like:

✔ **Being honest with God about how we feel.**
✔ **Trusting Him, even when we don't understand.**
✔ **Choosing His will over our own.**

Why Surrendering to God Brings Freedom

Holding on to control is exhausting. It creates stress, anxiety, and fear. But when we surrender, we exchange:

✔**Worry for peace.** (*Philippians 4:6–7*)
✔**Our plans for His perfect will.** (*Proverbs 3:5–6*)
✔**Our strength for His power.** (*2 Corinthians 12:9*)

God is not asking us to figure everything out—He's asking us to trust Him.

How to Pray Prayers of Surrender

If surrender feels difficult, here's a simple way to start:

1. **Acknowledge that you're struggling to let go.**
2. **Tell God what you're afraid of.**
3. **Release it to Him, trusting that He knows best.**

Guided Prayer: Letting Go

"Father, I confess that I like to be in control. I want to know what's coming next, and I struggle to trust You when life feels uncertain. But today, I choose

to surrender. I give You my fears, my plans, and my future. Not my will, but Yours be done. Amen."

Reflection Question

➡ **What is one area of your life that you need to surrender to God today?**

Testimony: How Letting Go Led to a Breakthrough

Frank the pilot had spent years trying to make everything work on his own. He had big dreams, big plans, and big expectations for how life should unfold.

He wanted control over everything—just like when he was in the cockpit of his jet. As an airline pilot, Frank was trained to manage every variable, anticipate every risk, and keep everything precisely on course. Altitude, speed, turbulence—all under control. He thrived on structure, order, and predictability. Life, he believed, should run just like a well-executed flight plan.

But when things started falling apart—his career, his finances, his relationships—he hit a breaking point.

"I realized I had been praying, but I was still trying to control everything. I wanted God to bless my plan instead of trusting His."

One night, feeling completely exhausted, he finally let go.

"I prayed, 'God, I'm done trying to force this. I give it all to You. Lead me wherever You want me to go.'"

The very next day, an unexpected call came—an opportunity that far exceeded anything Frank had imagined. It was as if the moment he let go, God began to unfold a plan far greater than his own.

In the weeks and months that followed, doors began to open—opportunities, relationships, and blessings—each one a reminder that what he couldn't control, **God could orchestrate perfectly.**

"I realized surrender doesn't mean giving up. It means making room for God to do something greater."

7

Praying Through Pain—Turning Wounds into Worship

How prayer helps us heal from hurt, grief, and disappointment.

Pain is a universal experience.

At some point, we all face loss, betrayal, heartbreak, disappointment, or deep grief.

When life hurts, prayer can feel impossible.
When the wounds are fresh, worship can feel forced.
When our hearts are broken, it can feel like God is silent.

But here's the truth: **God meets us in our pain.**

In our tears, He is there.
In our questions, He is listening.
In our brokenness, He is healing.

The Bible is filled with people who prayed through pain, sorrow, and suffering—and in doing so, they found healing.
And so can we.

Jesus' Example: Praying Through Pain

Jesus knew pain.

✔ He wept when His friend Lazarus died. (*John 11:35*)
✔ He was betrayed by someone He loved. (*Luke 22:47–48*)
✔ He felt abandoned in His darkest moment. (*Matthew 27:46*)

And what did He do in His deepest suffering? **He prayed.**

In the Garden of Gethsemane, Jesus fell on His face before the Father and poured out His pain:

"Father, if You are willing, take this cup from Me; yet not My will, but Yours be done." — *Luke 22:42*

Jesus didn't hide His pain.
He didn't pretend everything was fine.
He brought His sorrow to the Father—and so should we.

Why Prayer Heals Our Hurt

1. Prayer Gives Us a Safe Place to Be Honest
• God is not afraid of our emotions.
• David prayed raw, unfiltered prayers in the Psalms—crying out in anger, sorrow, and confusion.

"I pour out my complaint before Him; before Him I tell my trouble." — *Psalm 142:2*

2. Prayer Shifts Our Focus from Pain to God's Presence
• When we fixate on our wounds, they grow deeper.
• When we focus on God, healing begins.

"The Lord is close to the brokenhearted and saves those who are crushed in spirit." — *Psalm 34:18*

3. Prayer Turns Wounds into Worship
• Worship is not denying our pain—it's declaring that God is still good, even in the middle of it.

"Though He slay me, yet will I hope in Him." — *Job 13:15*

4. Prayer Helps Us Surrender Our Pain to God
• Healing happens when we release our pain into His hands.

"Cast all your anxiety on Him because He cares for you." — *1 Peter 5:7*

How to Pray Through Pain

When you're hurting, pray like this:

1. Tell God Exactly How You Feel

"Father, I don't understand. This hurts. I feel lost. But I come to You with my broken heart."

2. Ask for His Comfort & Healing

"Lord, I need Your presence. Wrap me in Your peace. Heal my wounds."

3. Surrender the Pain to Him

"I don't have the strength to carry this, so I give it to You. Take my grief, my sorrow, and my disappointment."

4. Declare Trust in His Plan

"Even in this pain, I trust You. Even when I don't see the good, I know You are working."

Guided Prayer: Lifting Up Your Hurt to God

"Father, You see my pain. You know the hurt I carry. I don't have the answers, but I know You are near. Help me to trust You, even in my grief. Heal my heart, restore my joy, and turn my pain into a testimony of Your faithfulness. In Jesus' name, Amen."

Reflection Question

➡ **What pain are you holding onto that you need to surrender to God today?**

Testimony: How Prayer Brought Healing After Heartbreak

Anna had been through deep betrayal.

The person she trusted most walked away, leaving her hurt, angry, and questioning God.

"I didn't want to pray," she said. *"I was too angry. Too broken."*

But one night, in desperation, she whispered a simple prayer:

"God, I don't even know what to say. But be with me Lord, when I am in trouble."

Over the next weeks, she kept praying—through the tears, the questions, and the frustration.

Slowly, her heart softened.
Gradually, peace replaced bitterness.
Eventually, she was able to forgive.

"I thought my pain would never go away. But as I kept bringing it to God, He healed me. The wounds didn't disappear overnight, but He walked with me through them. And now, I can say—He is still good, even after the hurt."

8

From Hate to Love—The Prayer That Changes Everything

How prayer transforms our hearts and helps us forgive.

Hurt has a way of turning into hate.

When someone wrongs us, betrays us, or deeply wounds us, the natural reaction is:

✔ **Anger** — They don't deserve forgiveness.
✔ **Bitterness** — I can never trust them again.
✔ **Resentment** — I won't let them get away with this.

But Jesus calls us to something radical:

"Love your enemies and pray for those who persecute you." — Matthew 5:44

That's not just a suggestion—it's a command.

Because the truth is, unforgiveness chains us to the past. But prayer?

✔ **Prayer softens our hearts.**
✔ **Prayer helps us let go of bitterness.**
✔ **Prayer frees us from the burden of hate.**

Forgiveness doesn't start with a feeling—it starts with a prayer.

Jesus' Example: Praying for His Enemies

No one experienced betrayal and injustice like Jesus:

✔ He was rejected by His own people. *(John 1:11)*
✔ He was abandoned by His closest friends. *(Matthew 26:56)*
✔ He was falsely accused, beaten, and nailed to a cross. *(Luke 23:33)*

And yet, in His darkest moment, He prayed for His enemies:

"Father, forgive them, for they do not know what they are doing." — Luke 23:34

Jesus had every right to be angry. He could have called down judgment—but instead, **He chose mercy.**

If Jesus could forgive the very people who crucified Him, what does that mean for us?

Why Forgiveness Begins with Prayer

Forgiveness isn't about excusing what happened—it's about freeing our hearts.

1. Prayer Helps Us Release the Pain
• Holding onto anger hurts us more than the person who wronged us.

"Get rid of all bitterness, rage, and anger... forgiving each other, just as in Christ God forgave you." — Ephesians 4:31–32

2. Prayer Softens Our Hearts
• It's impossible to hate someone you are genuinely praying for.

"Bless those who curse you, pray for those who mistreat you." — Luke 6:28

3. Prayer Shifts Our Focus from Hurt to Healing
• Instead of reliving the pain, we surrender it to God.

"Cast all your anxiety on Him because He cares for you." — 1 Peter 5:7

How to Pray Through Unforgiveness

If you're struggling to forgive, start here:

1. Be Honest with God

"Lord, this person hurt me. I don't want to forgive, but I know You call me to."

2. Ask God for the Strength to Forgive

"I can't do this alone. Soften my heart. Help me see them the way You see them."

3. Pray for the Person Who Hurt You

"Bless them, Lord. Heal them. Let them experience Your love."

At first, you might not feel anything. That's okay.
Forgiveness isn't a one-time moment—it's a daily decision.
But the more you pray, the freer you become.

Prayer for Forgiveness

"Father, I bring my pain to You. I don't want to hate anymore or hold onto bitterness anymore. Help me to forgive and love more, just as You always forgive me and always love me. Soften my heart, heal my wounds, and free me from hate. I choose love over hate, mercy over judgment. In Jesus' name, Amen."

Reflection Question

➡ **Is there someone you hate—someone you need to forgive today? Can you start by praying for them?**

Testimony: How Prayer Helped Me Forgive the Unforgivable

This is a snippet from Frank's book *"From Hate to Love."*

At Embry-Riddle Aeronautical University, *Advanced Aerodynamics II* was a really tough class, and Frank had to study night and day just to get a C grade. However, Doug would only have to see, hear, or read the course material and formulas once and he knew the material. He barely studied for any exams, and yet he obtained an A grade.

Frank was jealous and envious of him, and a feeling of hate within Frank grew toward him during that semester.

"Why did I have to study so hard and he barely spent any time studying? That wasn't fair."

Frank carried that hatred toward Doug throughout college, leaving wounds that never healed.

"I told myself I didn't care. But deep down, the hatred was still there."

One day, during a sermon on forgiveness, he felt God whisper: **"Pray for him."**

At first, Frank resisted. *Why should I pray for someone who did better than me and worked less for it?*

But he took a step of obedience.

"At first, I could barely say the words. But I kept praying—every day."

Over time, something shifted. His heart softened. The hate faded. And one day, he found himself wanting to reach out.

Years later, Frank and Doug reconnected. Eventually Frank learned that Doug had a photographic memory—a rare ability to remember information and visual images in great detail.

Once Frank fully comprehended and accepted this special skill of Doug's, Frank forgave him. Soon thereafter, Frank also forgave himself—for disliking his friend just because he had skills Frank did not have.

He realized that **God gave Doug certain gifts, and God gave him others.** Through prayer, Frank chose to accept this and move on.

His heart was free.

"Forgiveness wasn't for Doug—it was for me."

9

Praying for Your Family—A Legacy of Faith

Interceding for loved ones and breaking generational chains.

If you want to leave behind something that truly lasts, **pray for your family.**

Money runs out. Success fades. Even the best plans can fall apart. But a foundation of faith—one built through prayer—will stand for generations.

Prayer has the power to break generational struggles, bring families closer, and lead loved ones to Jesus. But many of us don't know where to start.

How do we pray for our families?
What if we're the only ones praying?
Can prayer really change what's happening in our homes?

Jesus showed us how.

Jesus' Example: Praying for Those He Loved

Jesus didn't just pray for Himself—**He constantly prayed for others.**

On the night before His crucifixion, He prayed not just for His disciples, but for all future believers—for people who had not yet come to know Him:

"I pray also for those who will believe in Me through their message, that all of them may be one, Father, just as You are in Me and I am in You."—John 17:20–21

That includes **us.**
Before we were even born, **Jesus was praying for us.**

If Jesus took time to pray for future generations, **shouldn't we do the same?**

The Power of Praying for Your Family

Praying for your family isn't about forcing change—it's about **inviting God to work.**

Here's what prayer can do in your home:

✔ **Prayer strengthens relationships.** (*Colossians 3:13–14*)
✔ **Prayer brings healing and restoration.** (*James 5:16*)
✔ **Prayer protects your loved ones.** (*Psalm 91:1*)
✔ **Prayer breaks generational struggles.** (*Exodus 20:6*)

Even when it feels like nothing is changing, know this: **God is always working.**

How to Pray for Your Family

If you want to start praying for your family but aren't sure how, try this:

1. Pray for their faith.
Ask God to draw them closer to Him.

2. Pray for their protection.
Ask God to cover them—physically, emotionally, and spiritually.

3. Pray for unity.
Ask God to strengthen relationships and bring peace to your home.

4. Pray for breakthrough.
Ask God to heal old wounds and bring transformation where it's needed.

Guided Prayer: Praying Over Your Family

"Father, thank You for the gift of family. Please protect and guide their thoughts, words, heart, and soul toward You during this earthly journey. Please help them to love God, themselves, and everyone. Protect them, and fill

their lives with Your peace. I love You, trust You, and believe in You. In Jesus' name, Amen."

Reflection Question

➡ **What is one specific way you can begin praying for your family today?**

Testimony: A Mother's Prayer That Changed Everything

For years, Maria prayed for her son.

He had grown up in church but drifted away in his teenage years. As he got older, he made choices that broke her heart.

"I wanted to fix him," she said, *"but I realized I couldn't."*

So, she prayed.

Day after day, she brought him before God. She didn't see change right away. In fact, things seemed to get worse. But she kept praying.

One night, her son called her—after years of avoiding conversations about faith.

"Mom, I don't know why, but I feel like I need to come back to God."

That night, he gave his life to Christ.

"Looking back," Maria says, *"I know my prayers didn't make the change —God did. But He used my prayers to work in my son's life, even when I couldn't see it."*

Section 3
Strengthening Your Prayer Life
Going Deeper in Spiritual Discipline.

10

Prayer and Fasting—Supercharging Your Spiritual Power

Unlocking the deeper power of fasting alongside prayer.

There are moments in life when ordinary prayers don't seem enough.

Times when we're desperate for a breakthrough, a deeper connection with God, or spiritual clarity.

In these moments, Jesus gave us a powerful tool: **fasting**.

Fasting is not just about going without food—it's about drawing closer to God. It's a way to say, *"Lord, You are my greatest need."*

When combined with prayer, fasting has the power to:

✔ **Break spiritual strongholds.** (*Isaiah 58:6*)
✔ **Bring clarity and direction.** (*Acts 13:2–3*)
✔ **Deepen our intimacy with God.** (*Matthew 4:2–4*)

Jesus prayed and fasted—and He invites us to do the same.

Jesus' Example: The Power of Fasting

Before Jesus began His ministry, He did something extraordinary —He fasted for forty days in the wilderness (*Matthew 4:1–2*).

Why?

Because **fasting prepares us for greater spiritual power.**

Satan tempted Jesus during His fast, but because He had been strengthened through prayer and fasting, He was able to overcome.

"Man shall not live by bread alone, but by every word that proceeds from the mouth of God." — Matthew 4:4

Jesus showed us that fasting is not about depriving ourselves—it's about **depending on God more than anything else.**

45

Why Should We Fast?

Fasting is a spiritual discipline that helps us:

✔ **Focus on God** – It removes distractions so we can hear Him clearly.

✔ **Increase spiritual strength** – It strengthens our ability to resist temptation.

✔ **Deepen our prayers** – Fasting shows God that we are serious about seeking Him.

✔ **Receive direction** – Many in the Bible fasted before making big decisions (*Acts 13:2–3*).

Types of Fasting

Not all fasts are the same. Here are some ways to fast:

1. Complete Fast – Abstaining from all food, drinking only water or liquids.

2. Partial Fast – Avoiding certain foods (like Daniel's fast of vegetables and water).

3. Intermittent Fast – Fasting for parts of the day (e.g., from sunrise to sunset).

4. Media/Social Fast – Abstaining from distractions like social media, TV, or entertainment to focus more on God.

The key is not what you give up—it's what you **replace it with**.

If you fast from food but don't spend time in prayer, it's just dieting.

If you fast from social media but don't seek God, it's just a break.

The power of fasting comes from replacing what we give up with more time in God's presence.

Originally, Frank created **Ten Healthy Tips** to help maintain a healthy human body and pass FAA Flight Medical Exams every six months—and to pass on these rules as survival tools to his children. However, he realized anyone can learn to live a healthier life utilizing these tips and later published the *Ten Healthy Tips* book.

Thinking, *if just one healthy tip helps one person in some way, then I'll be happily rewarded, and my lifelong goal to help mankind will be fulfilled.*

Fasting is a big part of Healthy Tip number six.

Fasting may be the single greatest natural healing therapy. It lowers the body's metabolism and helps remove toxins and waste from the body. Fasting is the avoidance of solid food and certain liquids. In a larger context, fasting is abstaining from that which is toxic to **mind, body, and soul**.

Fasting can also involve removing oneself from worldly responsibilities, embracing complete silence, and even social isolation.

How to Start Fasting

1. Start small – Try skipping one meal and using that time for prayer.
2. Pray before you fast – Ask God to guide you in how and when to fast.
3. Stay spiritually engaged – Spend time reading the Bible, praying, and worshiping.
4. Break the fast wisely – If fasting food, ease back into eating gently.

Guided Prayer: Asking for Strength to Fast

"Father, I want to seek You more deeply. Teach me to fast in a way that brings me closer to You. Give me strength, focus, and a hunger for Your presence above all else. Let my fasting bring spiritual breakthrough. In Jesus' name, Amen."

Reflection Question

➡ **What is one thing you can fast from this week to deepen your connection with God?**

Testimony: A Fast That Brought Breakthrough

Daniel had been praying for a job breakthrough for months, but nothing was happening.

"I felt stuck," he said. *"I was praying, but I wasn't hearing from God."*

One day, he felt God leading him to fast. He decided to fast from lunch each day for a week—using that time to pray and seek God instead.

By the fourth day, something changed.

"I felt God speaking to me—telling me to apply for a job I hadn't considered before."

He applied, got an interview, and within a week, he had the job.

"It wasn't about the job—it was about what happened inside of me," Daniel said. *"Fasting helped me get out of my own way and hear God more clearly."*

11

Hearing God's Voice—How to Recognize His Guidance in Prayer

Understanding how God speaks and how to listen.

Prayer is not just about talking to God—it's about **hearing from Him too.**

Many people wonder:

✔ How do I know if God is speaking to me?
✔What if I'm just hearing my own thoughts?
✔Does God still speak today?

The answer is **yes.**

God speaks to His people—not just pastors, prophets, or spiritual leaders, but **everyone who seeks Him.**

"My sheep listen to My voice; I know them, and they follow Me." — John 10:27

The problem is not that God isn't speaking—it's that we're not always listening.

So how do we recognize His voice?

Jesus' Example: Taking Time to Listen

Jesus didn't just pray and move on—He spent time in silence, **listening to the Father.**

✔ Before choosing His disciples, He prayed all night. (*Luke 6:12–13*)
✔ Before facing the cross, He listened for the Father's will. (*Luke 22:42*)
✔ He only did what He saw the Father doing. (*John 5:19*)

If Jesus, the Son of God, needed quiet time to hear from the Father, **how much more do we?**

How Does God Speak?

God speaks in different ways:

1. Through Scripture
• God's Word is His primary voice. If something contradicts Scripture, it's not from God.

"Your word is a lamp for my feet, a light on my path." — Psalm 119:105

2. Through the Holy Spirit
• Sometimes, God speaks through a deep inner knowing—a conviction in our spirit.

"When the Spirit of truth comes, He will guide you into all truth." — John 16:13

3. Through Peace or Unease
• God often leads us through peace (when we're in His will) or unease (when we're not).

"Let the peace of Christ rule in your hearts." — Colossians 3:15

4. Through Wise Counsel
• God speaks through trusted spiritual mentors, pastors, and godly friends.

"Plans fail for lack of counsel, but with many advisers they succeed." — Proverbs 15:22

5. Through Circumstances
• Sometimes, doors open or close in ways that make it clear where God is leading.

"In their hearts humans plan their course, but the Lord establishes their steps." — Proverbs 16:9

How to Hear God's Voice More Clearly

If you struggle to hear God's voice, here's how to become more sensitive to His leading:

1. Spend Time in God's Word
• The more we know Scripture, the more we recognize His voice.

2. Create Silence in Your Prayer Time
• After you pray, pause and listen instead of rushing to the next thing.

3. Ask God to Speak
• Pray: *"Lord, I want to hear Your voice. Speak to me today."*

4. Pay Attention to Repeated Messages
• If God is trying to get your attention, you may hear the same message multiple times—through Scripture, people, or sermons.

Guided Prayer: Asking God to Speak

"O my dear God, I want to hear Your voice. Help me to find meaning and purpose in life. Help me to recognize when You are speaking. Open my heart to Your guidance, and teach me to listen. Let Your voice be clear in my life. I love You, trust You, and believe in You. Amen."

Reflection Question

➡ **When was the last time you felt God speaking to you? If you haven't noticed, how can you slow down and listen?**

Testimony: How I Learned to Recognize God's Voice

John, an airline pilot, had been praying for meaning and purpose in his life.

"I kept asking God, 'Show me what to do,' but I felt like I wasn't getting an answer."

John had flown planes all over the world, but he had always felt like something was missing.

One day, John was soaring over the vast expanse of the ocean, and he had an experience that shook him to his core. As he piloted the aircraft, a supernatural and awe-inspiring feeling enveloped him, and suddenly, he heard a voice resounding within

51

him—a voice that he instinctively recognized as the unmistakable voice of God.

God spoke these words to him: *"John, your job is to love."*

About a month after his spiritual encounter with God, John was diagnosed with necrotizing fasciitis. He entered into a coma. On day four, after extensive treatment and care from medical professionals, John finally emerged from his coma. *(The long version of this story is in Frank's book "God Said to Me.")*

"The Lord will guide you always." — *Isaiah 58:11*

"God wasn't silent—I just needed to slow down and pay attention to how He was speaking."

12

Praying Boldly—Asking for More Without Fear

Building faith to pray bigger prayers with confidence.

Many of us pray small prayers because we don't want to be disappointed.

We ask for just enough instead of believing for the impossible.

But Jesus never told us to play it safe in prayer. Instead, He invited us to pray **boldly, fearlessly, and expectantly.**

"Ask, and it will be given to you; seek, and you will find; knock, and the door will be opened to you." — *Matthew 7:7*

When Jesus spoke these words, He didn't say:

✔ *"Ask for small things."*
✔ *"Seek only what seems reasonable."*
✔ *"Knock quietly and hope someone answers."*

He simply said: **ASK. SEEK. KNOCK.**
And He promised God would respond.

Jesus' Example: Bold Prayers, Big Miracles

Jesus never prayed timidly.

✔ He prayed for **Lazarus to rise from the dead.** (*John 11:41–44*)
✔ He prayed for **five loaves and two fish to feed thousands.** (*Matthew 14:19–20*)
✔ He prayed for His disciples to **receive power to change the world.** (*John 17:20–21*)

He didn't hope for small results—He expected big things.

And He told us to do the same:

"Truly I tell you, anyone who believes in Me will do the works I have been doing, and they will do even greater things than these." — *John 14:12*

Jesus was saying:

- ✔ Pray for **miracles**.
- ✔ Pray for **transformation**.
- ✔ Pray with **expectation**.

When we pray boldly, we show that we truly believe in the **power of God**.

What Holds Us Back from Praying Boldly?

1. **Fear of Disappointment**
   - *"What if I pray and nothing happens?"*
   - *"What if God doesn't answer the way I want?"*

2. **Thinking We're Asking for Too Much**
   - *"God has bigger things to worry about."*
   - *"Maybe I should just be grateful for what I have."*

3. **Doubting We Deserve It**
   - *"I haven't been a perfect Christian."*
   - *"Why would God answer my prayers?"*

But Jesus never placed limits on what we could ask for. Instead, He said:

"You do not have because you do not ask." — *James 4:2*

How to Pray Boldly Without Fear

1. Believe that God is able

"Now to Him who is able to do immeasurably more than all we ask or imagine." — *Ephesians 3:20*

2. Pray bigger than what seems possible

- Stop praying safe, small prayers—start praying **faith-filled prayers**.

3. Keep praying, even when you don't see answers right away
• Bold prayers require **bold persistence** (*Luke 18:1*).

4. Trust that God's answer is always for your good
• If He says **"yes,"** it's for your good.
• If He says **"wait,"** it's for your good.
• If He says **"no,"** it's because He has something even better.

Guided Prayer: Asking with Boldness

"Father, I come to You with bold faith today. You are a God of miracles, and I trust that nothing is too big for You. I bring my requests before You, believing that You hear me and will answer in Your perfect way. Help me to pray without fear, without limits, and with complete trust in Your goodness. In Jesus' name, Amen."

Reflection Question

➡ **What is one bold prayer you've been afraid to pray? Can you bring it to God today?**

Testimony: A Bold Prayer That Changed Everything

Jasmine had always been afraid to pray big prayers.

"I didn't want to be disappointed," she said. *"I told myself that I didn't need much—I just needed to get by."*

Then one day, a friend challenged her:

"What if God wants to do more in your life than just 'get you by'?"

So, she started praying differently.

Instead of asking for *"just enough"*, she prayed for **overflow**—for her finances, her dreams, and her ability to bless others.

Within months, she was offered a higher-paying job than she ever thought possible. A side business she had started unexpectedly took off.

"It wasn't about the money," she said. *"It was about realizing that I had been shrinking my prayers because I was afraid. Now, I pray boldly, because I know my God is big."*

13

The Prayer That Moves Mountains—Unlocking Miracles Through Prayer

How to pray for breakthroughs and expect results.

Some prayers feel ordinary. Others feel impossible.

We all face situations that seem too big, too hopeless, too unchangeable. A diagnosis that doctors say won't improve. A financial crisis that has no solution. A relationship that seems beyond repair.

But Jesus made a bold promise about prayer—one that sounds almost too good to be true:

"Truly I tell you, if you have faith as small as a mustard seed, you can say to this mountain, 'Move from here to there,' and it will move. Nothing will be impossible for you." — *Matthew 17:20*

Mountains represent the impossible obstacles in our lives. And Jesus is telling us that through **faith-filled prayer**, even the biggest mountains can move.

But how?

How do we pray the kind of prayers that move mountains?

Jesus' Example: Praying with Bold Faith

Jesus constantly prayed for miracles—and **He expected them to happen.**

✔ He prayed for the blind to see—and they did. (*Matthew 20:32–34*)
✔ He prayed over food—and it multiplied. (*Matthew 14:19*)
✔ He prayed for the dead to rise—and they did. (*John 11:41–44*)

He didn't just wish for miracles. **He prayed, believed, and acted.**

And He taught His disciples to do the same:

"Whatever you ask for in prayer, believe that you have received it, and it will be yours." — Mark 11:24

What Stops Our Mountains from Moving?

Many of us pray safe prayers because we're afraid of disappointment.
We ask for what feels possible rather than what requires faith.

But Jesus tells us there are two things that can stop our mountains from moving:

1. Doubt

"But when you ask, you must believe and not doubt." — James 1:6

2. Lack of Persistence

"They should always pray and not give up." — Luke 18:1

Mountain-moving prayers require faith and persistence.
Faith believes that God CAN.
Persistence refuses to stop praying until He DOES.

How to Pray Mountain-Moving Prayers

If you're facing something that feels impossible, here's how to pray with the kind of faith that Jesus taught:

1. Pray Specifically
• Instead of praying, *"God, help me,"* pray boldly and clearly:
• *"God, I believe You can heal my body."*
• *"God, I trust You to restore my marriage."*

2. Pray with Faith, Not Fear
• Speak God's promises over your situation.
• If Jesus said, *"Nothing is impossible with God"* (*Luke 1:37*), then pray like you believe it.

3. Pray Until Something Happens
• Some prayers are answered instantly—others require consistent faith.
• Keep praying. Keep believing. Keep trusting.

4. Take Action
• Faith isn't just believing—it's acting.
• If you're praying for a job, apply for one.
• If you're praying for a breakthrough, walk in obedience.

Guided Prayer: Asking for a Miracle

"Father, I come to You with bold faith. You are the God who moves mountains, and I believe nothing is impossible for You. I bring this situation before You, trusting that You can do more than I can imagine. Strengthen my faith. Help me to keep praying and believing, no matter how long it takes. In Jesus' name, Amen."

Reflection Question

➡ **What is the biggest "mountain" in your life right now? How can you pray boldly about it?**

Testimony: When a Mountain Moved

Jordan had been praying for his brother for 10 years.

His brother had walked away from God, refused to talk about faith, and seemed further from Jesus than ever.

"I almost gave up," Jordan admitted. *"I kept thinking, maybe this is just how it is."*

But something in his heart told him to keep praying.

One night, out of nowhere, his brother called him:

"I don't know why, but I feel like I need to come back to God. Can we talk?"

It wasn't a coincidence.
It wasn't random.
It was a **mountain-moving prayer** answered in God's perfect timing.

Section 4

Sacred Traditions and Powerful Prayer Practices

Deepening Your Relationship with God Through Time-Honored Devotions.

14

Timeless Paths of Prayer: Prophets, Religions, and Their Spiritual Wisdom

Discover how the great spiritual traditions and prophetic voices can enrich your prayer life.

We are not the first to seek God.

For thousands of years, across every continent and culture, people have turned their hearts toward the heavens—asking, listening, and longing for connection with the Divine. **Prayer is not new.** It is ancient, sacred, and woven into the human story.

What if we could learn from the prayers of those who came before us? What if the voices of prophets, saints, and seekers from different traditions could inspire us to go deeper with God today?

This chapter is an invitation to explore the richness of global prayer traditions—not to replace our personal relationship with Jesus, but to see how prayer has always been a bridge between the human heart and God's heart.

Prayer Across the World: A Shared Spiritual Thread

Here are some of the world's major faith traditions and how they express prayer:

• **Christianity** — Prayer is personal, powerful, and relational. From The Lord's Prayer to spontaneous worship, prayer connects believers to God through Christ.
• **Islam** — Muslims pray five times daily, facing Mecca, in a disciplined rhythm of worship and surrender.
• **Hinduism** — Prayer includes chants, mantras, and offerings— invoking divine energy and aligning with spiritual truths.
• **Buddhism** — Meditation and loving-kindness prayers (Metta)

foster compassion and spiritual clarity.

• **Judaism** — Prayer is both individual and communal, with sacred texts like the Shema and the Amidah shaping devotion.

• **Sikhism** — Prayer is offered through hymns and scripture readings, with a strong emphasis on meditating on God's name.

• **Indigenous and Folk Religions** — Often emphasize nature-based rituals, honoring ancestors, and connecting to the spiritual world.

• **Bahá'í Faith** — Daily prayers emphasize unity, peace, and personal communion with God.

Though these traditions differ in form, they all reflect one truth: **Human hearts long for divine connection.**

Prayers That Have Stood the Test of Time

These iconic prayers, spoken by millions across generations, still resonate today:

• **The Lord's Prayer** (*Christianity*) — Taught by Jesus Himself, this is the foundation of Christian prayer, covering worship, surrender, provision, forgiveness, and protection.

• **The Hail Mary** (*Catholic Christianity*) — A powerful plea for intercession and grace through the Blessed Mother.

• **The Shahada** (*Islam*) — A declaration of God's oneness and the prophetic role of Muhammad.

• **The Shema** (*Judaism*) — A bold proclamation of God's singular sovereignty.

• **The Serenity Prayer** (*Interfaith*) — A comforting cry for peace, courage, and wisdom.

• **The Gayatri Mantra** (*Hinduism*) — A prayer for divine illumination and wisdom.

• **The Metta Prayer** (*Buddhism*) — A heartfelt offering of peace and love for all beings.

• **The Amidah** (*Judaism*) — A deeply reverent prayer of thanksgiving, praise, and petition.

• **The Jesus Prayer** (*Eastern Orthodoxy*) — A meditative call for mercy and intimacy with Christ.

• **The Prayer of St. Francis** (*Christianity*) — A selfless invitation to be a vessel of peace, love, and service.

These prayers are more than words—they are **spiritual doorways**. Each one carries centuries of faith, devotion, and divine encounter.

Why These Prayers Still Matter Today

You may wonder: *What can I learn from ancient prayers when I already talk to God in my own way?*

The answer is simple: **Depth and diversity can strengthen your spiritual life.**

• They broaden your understanding of how people relate to God.
• They teach reverence and structure without replacing spontaneity.
• They connect you to generations of faith who have walked this path before you.
• They remind you that prayer is bigger than your moment—it's part of a timeless movement.

A Prayerful Reflection

"Father, I thank You for the voices of those who have gone before me. Teach me to pray with the same reverence, passion, and boldness. Help me learn from their devotion and deepen my own walk with You. Let their words ignite my spirit, and may my prayers echo into eternity. Amen."

Reflection Question

➡ **Which traditional prayer speaks to your heart today—and how can you incorporate its spirit into your own prayer life?**

Testimony: How Ancient Prayers Deepened My Faith

Tom had grown up in a modern church setting—comfortable, casual, and full of freedom. But something felt missing.

"I loved praying freely, but sometimes I didn't know what to say," he shared.

One day, he stumbled across **The Prayer of St. Francis** in an old devotional book. Something stirred in him.

"I started praying it daily, and it began to change me. It wasn't just the words —it was the posture of humility and love."

Later, he began exploring other traditional prayers like **The Lord's Prayer** and **The Jesus Prayer**.

"They gave me language for my soul. They grounded me."

Now, Tom says he blends spontaneous prayer with sacred tradition—and **his prayer life has never been more alive.**

15

Walking with Mary: Embracing Deeper Prayer through Her Help and Intercession

Inviting the Blessed Mother into your prayer journey for comfort, strength, and spiritual growth.

There are many Christian faith traditions, and while most Christians acknowledge **Mary as the mother of Jesus Christ**, not all embrace the idea of seeking her intercession. Some worry that devotion to Mary may overshadow their personal relationship with Jesus, who is both fully God and fully man, while Mary remains fully human. Others believe Mary plays no role in God's plan of salvation through Jesus.

However, **I believe Mary can serve as a beautiful and loving intercessor**—our spiritual "middlewoman" who brings our petitions to her Son. Jesus, like most children, delights in pleasing His mother. Developing a deeper relationship with Mary naturally leads us closer to Jesus, her Son.

Consider the story of the **wedding at Cana**. When the hosts ran out of wine, it was Mary who noticed and brought the concern to Jesus. Although His time had not yet come, He honored her request and performed His first public miracle.

If Mary cared about something as simple as wine at a wedding, how much more would she care about the deeper needs of your heart?

So, pray. Beg. Plead. Ask Mary to bring your requests before Jesus. **She is eager to help.** I once read a statement—though I can't recall its source—that *Mary has more grace blessings to give than the number of people requesting them.* That truth has stayed with me ever since.

Mary is overflowing with graces and spiritual gifts, just waiting for us to ask. These blessings can be offered for anyone

—whether you love them or not, whether you know them or not. You can pray for those who uplift you, and especially for those who challenge you.

If someone is aggravating you, testing your patience, or bringing you distress—don't respond with bitterness. **Offer a grace blessing instead.** Visualize your prayer as a beam of light, like a spiritual laser reaching their heart. Even in moments of conflict, you can speak a grace blessing silently in your heart or out loud if appropriate. A loving response can be more powerful than a harsh word.

The Grace Blessing Prayer

Here's a simple and powerful tool I use, which I call the **Grace Blessing Prayer.** You can personalize it with the name of the person you're praying for. If the moment allows, and with their permission, you may gently place your hand on their forehead and say:

"Hail Mary, full of grace, open up your hands and shine a ray of grace onto [Name]."

Feel free to adapt this prayer for your own use:

GRACE BLESSING

Hail Mary, full of grace, open up your hands and shine a ray of grace onto

_____.

Mary's Global Presence: A History of Apparitions

Mary's love and intercession have been revealed in extraordinary ways across the world. Over **300 Marian apparitions** have been recorded in various countries and cultures, offering hope, healing, and messages of conversion.

Here are some of the most well-known Marian apparitions:

• **Our Lady of Guadalupe** (*Mexico, 1531*)
Visionary: St. Juan Diego
Message: Love, compassion, and conversion
Significance: Her miraculous image on Juan Diego's tilma remains a powerful symbol of faith and divine presence.

• **Our Lady of Lourdes** (*France, 1858*)
Visionary: St. Bernadette Soubirous
Message: Prayer, penance, and healing
Significance: The healing spring at Lourdes is a source of miraculous cures and spiritual renewal.

• **Our Lady of Fátima** (*Portugal, 1917*)
Visionaries: Lucia, Jacinta, and Francisco Marto
Message: Pray the Rosary, repentance, and conversion
Significance: The Three Secrets of Fátima and the Miracle of the Sun touched hearts worldwide.

• **Our Lady of Knock** (*Ireland, 1879*)
Visionaries: 15 villagers
Message: A silent yet profound message of presence and hope
Significance: Appeared with St. Joseph and St. John the Evangelist, offering quiet reassurance in a time of hardship.

• **Our Lady of La Salette** (*France, 1846*)
Visionaries: Maximin Giraud and Mélanie Calvat
Message: Call to repentance, respect for the Sabbath, and avoiding blasphemy
Significance: Mary weeping showed deep sorrow for humanity's sins.

• **Our Lady of Zeitoun** (*Egypt, 1968–1971*)
Visionaries: Witnessed by thousands across faiths
Message: Unity and peace
Significance: A rare mass apparition seen by Muslims and Christians alike.

• **Our Lady of Beauraing** (*Belgium, 1932–1933*)
Visionaries: Five children
Message: Prayer and devotion to the Immaculate Heart
Significance: Known as "the Virgin with the Golden Heart."

• **Our Lady of Banneux** (*Belgium, 1933*)
Visionary: Mariette Beco
Message: *"I am the Virgin of the Poor"* — a call to faith and healing
Significance: A compassionate reminder that Mary intercedes for the suffering.

These apparitions remind us that **Mary is not distant—she walks with us**, ready to guide, intercede, and bless. Through her, we deepen our connection to Jesus.

Let your prayer journey be enriched by her loving presence.

16

The Power of the Rosary: A Prayer that Echoes Through the Ages

Explore the beauty and transformative power of praying the Rosary daily.

If you want to embrace one of the most powerful and sacred prayer experiences, immerse yourself in the **Holy Rosary**—a devotional prayer that echoes through centuries and hearts. The Rosary is not just a routine of words—it is a **spiritual journey**, a meditative walk through the life, death, and resurrection of Jesus Christ, guided by the loving intercession of His mother, the Blessed Virgin Mary.

This sacred prayer has been a spiritual anchor for countless souls, offering **peace in turmoil, strength in weakness, and clarity in confusion**. Through it, we grow closer to Jesus by walking hand-in-hand with Mary, contemplating the profound mysteries of Christ's love.

A Brief History of the Rosary

The origins of the Rosary trace back to the early centuries of Christian monasticism, when monks recited the 150 Psalms. Since most laypeople could not read or memorize all the Psalms, a simplified prayer practice evolved—repeating **150 Hail Marys in groups of ten**, with the Our Father in between.

Tradition holds that in the 13th century, the **Blessed Virgin Mary appeared to St. Dominic**, giving him the Rosary as a spiritual weapon to combat heresy and bring about conversion. This devotion gradually took form and structure over the years, especially under the influence of the **Dominican Order**. By the 16th century, the Rosary had become the structured prayer we recognize today.

Pope St. John Paul II deepened this tradition by introducing the **Luminous Mysteries** in 2002, focusing on the public ministry of Jesus and enriching the prayer even further.

Why Pray the Rosary?

The Rosary is much more than repetition—it is **contemplation**. As your lips speak the familiar prayers, your heart reflects on the sacred mysteries—moments of Christ's life that reveal His love and purpose. In a noisy, chaotic world, the Rosary provides a rhythmic, calming cadence that draws your soul into stillness and divine encounter.

People around the world pray the Rosary for many reasons:

• Personal transformation
• Inner peace and healing
• Intercession for loved ones
• Spiritual protection
• Guidance and discernment
• Thanksgiving and praise

How to Pray the Rosary: A Step-by-Step Guide

1. Begin with the Sign of the Cross
2. Apostles' Creed – A profession of your faith.
3. Our Father – The prayer Jesus taught us.
4. Three Hail Marys – Offered for an increase in faith, hope, and charity.
5. Glory Be – A doxology glorifying the Trinity.

Then pray the **Five Decades**, each consisting of:

• One Our Father
• Ten Hail Marys
• One Glory Be
• *(Optional)* The **Fatima Prayer**: *"O my Jesus, forgive us our sins, save us from the fires of hell, lead all souls to heaven, especially those in most need of thy mercy."*

6. Conclude with the Hail Holy Queen, and any additional concluding prayers like the Rosary Prayer or the **Litany of the Blessed Virgin Mary.**

The Mysteries of the Rosary

Each day of the week traditionally focuses on one set of Mysteries—each set reflecting powerful scenes from Jesus' life and mission:

Joyful Mysteries (Mondays & Saturdays)
– The Annunciation
– The Visitation
– The Nativity
– The Presentation in the Temple
– The Finding of Jesus in the Temple

Sorrowful Mysteries (Tuesdays & Fridays)
– The Agony in the Garden
– The Scourging at the Pillar
– The Crowning with Thorns
– The Carrying of the Cross
– The Crucifixion and Death of Jesus

Glorious Mysteries (Wednesdays & Sundays)
– The Resurrection
– The Ascension
– The Descent of the Holy Spirit
– The Assumption of Mary
– The Coronation of Mary as Queen of Heaven and Earth

Luminous Mysteries (Thursdays) *(Introduced by Pope St. John Paul II)*
– The Baptism of Jesus in the Jordan
– The Wedding Feast at Cana
– The Proclamation of the Kingdom of God
– The Transfiguration
– The Institution of the Holy Eucharist

A Prayer that Changes You

The Rosary is more than a prayer—it's a **weapon against darkness**, a **balm for the soul**, and a **doorway into divine intimacy**. When prayed daily with devotion, it has the power to **soften hardened hearts, heal brokenness, protect families**, and draw entire lives into the light of Christ's mercy and love.

As you hold each bead and whisper each prayer, remember that you are not just praying—you are **inviting heaven to enter your life**. You are walking with Mary and gazing upon Jesus.

Let this prayer become part of your rhythm, your refuge, and your relationship with God.

17

Novenas: The Strength of Nine Days of Intentional Prayer

Experience spiritual breakthroughs through focused, intentional nine-day prayers.

A **novena** is a powerful and sacred form of prayer in the Christian tradition, prayed over nine consecutive days to seek a special grace, intercession, or divine intervention. The word *novena* comes from the Latin *novem*, meaning **nine**. This practice symbolizes **spiritual perseverance** and mirrors the nine days the Apostles and the Blessed Virgin Mary spent in prayer after Jesus' Ascension, leading up to the descent of the Holy Spirit at **Pentecost**.

Novenas help deepen faith, bring clarity in times of uncertainty, and open hearts to God's will. Whether you're seeking healing, peace, strength, or a miracle, novenas invite you into a deeper rhythm of **intentional prayer**, allowing God to work in His time and in His way.

Popular and Powerful Novenas

While there are countless novenas for different saints, devotions, and intentions, here are five of the most beloved and widely-prayed novenas in the Christian tradition:

1. Novena to the Sacred Heart of Jesus
• Focus: Deep devotion to the merciful love of Jesus' heart.
• Purpose: Prayed for healing, spiritual renewal, and special intentions.
• Duration: 9 days, often ending on the Feast of the Sacred Heart.
• Spiritual Impact: Invites you into the tender, compassionate heart of Christ.

2. Novena to Our Lady of Perpetual Help
• Focus: Mary's maternal care and protection.
• Purpose: Often used for urgent needs, comfort during trials, and healing.
• Tradition: Prayed individually or in groups—some churches pray it weekly.

3. Novena to St. Jude (Patron of Hopeless Cases)
• Focus: Help in impossible or desperate situations.
• Purpose: One of the most popular novenas worldwide, prayed for miracles and hope when all seems lost.
• Known for: Bringing comfort to hearts in crisis and reminding us that nothing is impossible with God

4. Novena to the Divine Mercy
• Focus: God's infinite mercy through Jesus.
• Purpose: Often prayed before Divine Mercy Sunday (the Sunday after Easter).
• Includes: The Divine Mercy Chaplet and special daily intentions.
• Message: "Jesus, I trust in You."

5. Novena to Our Lady of the Miraculous Medal
• Focus: Mary's special intercession through the Miraculous Medal.
• Purpose: Prayed for physical and spiritual blessings, conversions, and protection.
• Belief: Those who wear the medal with faith receive abundant graces through Mary's care.

Find a Saint That Speaks to You

Because of my name, I feel a special connection to **St. Francis of Assisi**. You might consider doing a little research on your own name—maybe you'll discover a saint or guardian angel whose life and virtues speak to your soul. Saints can serve as powerful intercessors and role models on your journey of faith.

Who Was St. Francis of Assisi?

- Lived from 1181–1226, born in Assisi, Italy.
- Known for his humility, love for the poor, radical simplicity, and reverence for all creation.
- Founded the Franciscan Order, embracing voluntary poverty to follow Jesus more closely.
- Patron saint of animals and ecology, beloved for his spirit of peace and joy.
- Received the stigmata, the wounds of Christ, as a mark of profound union with Jesus
- Credited with creating the first nativity scene in 1223 in Greccio, Italy—bringing the humble birth of Jesus to life in a tangible, emotional way.

St. Francis of Assisi Novena—A Prayer of Simplicity and Peace

This novena is a beautiful way to seek St. Francis' intercession for peace, healing, humility, and a deeper love for God and creation. Each day has a special theme to help you grow in virtue and closeness to Christ.

Daily Structure: • Sign of the Cross
• Opening Prayer:

O beloved St. Francis, gentle and humble servant of the Most High, you left behind all earthly comforts to follow Christ in perfect poverty and joy. Teach us to live with simplicity, peace, and compassion. Pray for us, that we may grow closer to Jesus and embrace God's will in all things. Amen.

Daily Petitions:
• Day 1 – Detachment from the World:
"St. Francis, help me seek treasures in heaven, not on earth."
• Day 2 – Peace of Heart:
"St. Francis, grant me inner peace and help me be an instrument of peace."
• Day 3 – Love for the Poor and Needy:
"St. Francis, help me see Christ in the poor and forgotten."
• Day 4 – Humility:
"St. Francis, teach me to be humble and serve with joy."

- **Day 5 – Love for Nature and All Creation:**
"St. Francis, inspire me to care for the earth and all God's creatures."
- **Day 6 – Joy in Suffering:**
"St. Francis, help me carry my cross with joy and faith."
- **Day 7 – Spirit of Prayer and Devotion:**
"St. Francis, draw me into deeper union with God through prayer."
- **Day 8 – Love for the Cross:**
"St. Francis, help me embrace sacrifice for love of Christ."
- **Day 9 – Holy Death and Eternal Life:**
"St. Francis, pray that I may live and die in God's grace."

Closing Prayer (Each Day):

St. Francis of Assisi, pray for us. Help us live the Gospel with joy and faithfulness. Through your intercession, may we become instruments of peace, healing, and love in the world. Amen.
(Add your personal intentions here)

Finish with:
- Our Father
- Hail Mary
- Glory Be

A Journey Worth Taking

Novenas offer us a sacred space to pour out our hearts to God with **focused faith, enduring trust, and deep hope**. Whether you are facing a challenge, longing for healing, or simply seeking to grow in holiness, a novena is a **spiritual journey worth taking—one prayer at a time, one day at a time.**

18

The Universal Prayer: A Call to Deeper Connection with God

Discover a powerful prayer that can center your spirit and draw you closer to God's heart.

Prayer is the breath of the soul. It is our daily conversation with God—a space of gratitude, surrender, and intimacy. While there are many traditional prayers that guide us in our faith, sometimes life calls for a simple, personal connection—one that flows straight from the heart.

I want to share with you a special prayer I wrote, a prayer I call **"Trinity for Me."** It became part of my spiritual rhythm during a season of intense challenge and pressure, and it continues to bless me today. I hope it becomes just as meaningful for you.

The Story Behind the Prayer

I began praying this during the summer of **2009**, when I was in intense flight training for a **captain's position on an Airbus wide-body jet aircraft**. The demands were overwhelming—long hours, limited sleep, and constant studying. Airline pilots are among the most rigorously trained and regulated professionals in the world.

Every six months, we must pass **federal simulator check rides**, preparing for emergency scenarios we hope never to encounter—but must be ready for, just in case. One well-known example of such a moment is **Captain Sully Sullenberger's "Miracle on the Hudson."** That kind of poise under pressure is what training is designed to prepare us for.

During those months, I barely had time to pray the traditional prayers. My days were consumed by technical systems, emergency drills, checklists, oral exams, written tests, simulator rides, and in-flight evaluations. I needed a prayer that was **simple, honest, and soul-centering**—something I could say quickly yet meaningfully, especially at night before I drifted off to sleep.

So, I created **"Trinity for Me"**—a prayer that captures both **gratitude and supplication** in a few heartfelt lines. At its core, it's a prayer of **thanks and trust**: *"Thank you for... and help me with..."*

TRINITY FOR ME

O my dear God
O my dear Jesus
And the Holy Spirit,
Thank You for this moment of life.
Thank You for this breath of air.
Thank You for providing water and food for my body,
And thank You for protecting, guiding, and nourishing my soul.
Thank You for _____.
Please help and/or grant me this request:

_____.
Please protect and guide my thoughts, words, heart, and soul
Toward You during this earthly journey, so that after this life I will be in heaven.
Please help me to love God, myself, and everyone.
I love You, trust You, believe in You, and hope to be with You.
Amen.

You can personalize this prayer—adjust the wording, fill in the blanks, or even write your own version inspired by it. Let it be a living prayer, one that grows with you through each season of your life.

The Lord's Prayer: Our Gold Standard

While personal prayers help us connect deeply with God, **Jesus Himself gave us the perfect prayer: the Lord's Prayer**, also known as the **Our Father**. It is the **gold standard**, taught by the Son of God as a model for all prayer:

Our Father, who art in heaven,
Hallowed be Thy name.
Thy kingdom come, Thy will be done,
On earth as it is in heaven.
Give us this day our daily bread,
And forgive us our trespasses,
As we forgive those who trespass against us.
And lead us not into temptation,
But deliver us from evil. Amen.

Start with the **Lord's Prayer**. Let it shape your heart. But also embrace the gift of **personal prayer**—like **"Trinity for Me"**—as an intimate offering of your heart to God.

May this prayer be a **lifeline in times of busyness**, a **source of calm in the storm**, and a **bridge between your heart and heaven**. In the quiet moments of your day—or in the final moments before sleep—may it draw you closer to the God who listens, loves, and walks beside you.

Create Your Own Prayer: A Personal Invitation to Intimacy with God

While traditional prayers provide structure and spiritual richness, your personal prayer is a sacred expression of your unique relationship with God. Just like the "Trinity for Me" prayer, you can create a prayer that flows from your heart, reflecting your gratitude, needs, hopes, and love.

There is no perfect formula—just sincerity. God isn't looking for fancy words; He's looking for your heart.

Take a moment now to **write your own prayer**. Use the prompts below if you need guidance, or simply let the words come naturally.

Prayer Writing Prompts:

- Begin by addressing God:
  "O God, my Father...," "Dear Jesus...," "Holy Spirit, my guide..."

- Express your gratitude:
  "Thank You for _____..."

- Share your needs, desires, or concerns:
  "Please help me with _____..."

- Ask for spiritual growth or strength:
  "Teach me to _____..."

- Offer your love and trust:
  "I trust You. I love You. I believe in You..."

- Close with a blessing or affirmation:
  "Amen." or *"May I walk in Your peace today and always."*

Your Prayer Journal Page:

(Use the space below to write your prayer. Let it be honest. Let it be you.)

markdown

Copyedit

_____

_____

_____

_____

_____

_____

_____

_____

_____

_____

_____

_____

_____

_____

_____

_____

_____

_____

_____

_____

Remember: prayer is not a performance—it's a relationship. Don't worry about the "right" words. God understands the language of your heart better than anyone else.

May this prayer-writing practice help you draw even closer to God's heart and deepen your daily connection with the divine.

19

Scripture and Prayer: Finding Prayer's Power in the New Testament

Explore where and how prayer is modeled throughout the life and teachings of Jesus and the Apostles.

Prayer is a central thread woven throughout the New Testament. Through the life of Jesus and the practices of His disciples, we are given powerful examples of what it means to pray with **sincerity, faith, and persistence.** Scripture reveals not only how to pray, but why prayer is essential in maintaining a **deep, intimate connection with God.**

Jesus Himself, the Son of God, prayed constantly—often retreating to quiet places to commune with the Father. His example invites us into a life where prayer is not an obligation, but a **lifeline**—where communication with God becomes the foundation of our spiritual journey.

Prayer in the Gospels: Jesus as Our Model

In the Gospel of Matthew: • *Matthew 6:5–13 – Teaching on Prayer and the Lord's Prayer:* Jesus teaches His disciples to pray with humility and sincerity, introducing what we now call the **Lord's Prayer,** a foundational guide for all Christian prayer.
• *Matthew 14:23 – Jesus Prays Alone:* After the miracle of feeding the five thousand, Jesus retreats to a mountain to pray alone, showing the importance of **solitude and personal communion** with God.
• *Matthew 26:36–44 – Prayer in Gethsemane:* In His moment of

anguish, Jesus prays fervently in the Garden of Gethsemane, **submitting to God's will** and showing the human depth of prayer during suffering.

In the Gospel of Mark: • *Mark 1:35 – Solitary Prayer:* Jesus rises early in the morning and goes to a quiet place to pray, emphasizing the value of **intentional time alone** with God.

• *Mark 6:46 – Prayer on the Mountain:* After ministry and miracles, Jesus again retreats for prayer, showing **balance between action and contemplation.**

• *Mark 14:32–42 – Gethsemane:* Jesus prays deeply before His arrest, **surrendering to God's will even in the face of unimaginable suffering.**

In the Gospel of Luke: Luke's Gospel uniquely highlights Jesus' prayer life more frequently than any other Gospel, underlining its importance in His ministry.

• *Luke 3:21–22 – Prayer at Baptism:* Jesus prays as He is baptized, and the Holy Spirit descends, affirming His divine identity.

• *Luke 5:16 – Praying in Solitude:* Jesus often withdraws to lonely places to pray, modeling **regular spiritual renewal.**

• *Luke 6:12–13 – Before Choosing the Apostles:* Jesus spends the entire night in prayer before selecting His twelve apostles, showing **discernment through prayer.**

• *Luke 9:18–20 – Before Peter's Confession:* Jesus prays before asking His disciples about His identity, preparing hearts for divine revelation.

• *Luke 9:28–29 – At the Transfiguration:* During prayer, Jesus' appearance changes, highlighting the **transformative power of prayer.**

• *Luke 11:1–4 – Teaching the Lord's Prayer:* A disciple asks Jesus to teach them to pray, prompting a second teaching of the Lord's Prayer.

• *Luke 22:31–32 – Praying for Peter's Faith:* Jesus tells Peter that He has personally prayed for his strength and perseverance.

• *Luke 22:39–46 – Prayer on the Mount of Olives:* Jesus prays in agony before His Passion, surrendering again to the Father's will.

• *Luke 23:34, 46 – Prayers from the Cross:* Even in death, Jesus prays —asking forgiveness for His persecutors and entrusting His spirit to God.

In the Gospel of John: • *John 11:41–42 – Before Raising Lazarus:* Jesus thanks God publicly, emphasizing **gratitude and trust** in God's response to prayer.

• *John 12:27–28 – Prayer in Distress:* Jesus expresses the weight of His coming suffering and seeks the Father's glorification.

• *John 17:1–26 – The High Priestly Prayer:* One of the most profound and intimate moments in Scripture, Jesus prays for:

  ○ Himself (John 17:1–5) – to be glorified and fulfill His mission.

  ○ His disciples (John 17:6–19) – for their protection and sanctification.

  ○ Future believers (John 17:20–26) – that all may be united in love and truth.

Prayer in the Early Church and Apostolic Letters

As we move beyond the Gospels, prayer continues to be a **cornerstone of Christian life** in the Acts of the Apostles and the letters of the New Testament. Prayer shaped the life of the early Church and was encouraged by the Apostles as a vital spiritual practice.

Jesus' Ongoing Intercession: • *Romans 8:34:* "It is Christ Jesus who died—yes, who was raised—who is at the right hand of God, who indeed intercedes for us."

• *Hebrews 7:25:* "Therefore He is able to save completely those who come to God through Him, because He always lives to intercede for them."

Teachings on Prayer: • *Romans 12:12:* "Rejoice in hope, be patient in suffering, persevere in prayer."

• *Ephesians 6:18:* "Pray in the Spirit at all times in every prayer and supplication. Keep alert and always persevere in supplication for all the saints."

• *Philippians 4:6:* "Do not worry about anything, but in everything by prayer and supplication with thanksgiving let your requests be made known to God."

• *1 Thessalonians 5:17:* "Pray without ceasing."

• *James 5:16:* "Confess your sins to one another, and pray for one another, so that you may be healed. The prayer of the righteous is powerful and effective."

Devotion to Prayer in the Early Church: • *Acts 2:42:* "They devoted themselves to the apostles' teaching and fellowship, to the breaking of bread and the prayers."

Prayer and Revelation: • *Revelation 1:1:* The book begins with the divine communication from Jesus Christ—a reminder that prayer is not just our reaching toward God, but **God also reaching toward us.**

A Living Legacy of Prayer

From Jesus' private moments with the Father to His passionate prayers for humanity, and from the early Church's communal devotion to the Apostles' exhortations—**prayer is a spiritual lifeline that sustains the Christian life.**

As you explore these scriptures, let them deepen your understanding of prayer's **purpose and power.** Let them encourage you to make prayer a daily habit, not just a ritual, but a **relationship**—a way of living with your heart always open to God.

As we've seen throughout the New Testament, prayer was not just an occasional activity—it was the **heartbeat of Jesus' life and the early Church.** Whether He was alone in a quiet place, surrounded by His disciples, or hanging on the cross, Jesus remained in constant communication with the Father.

His example teaches us something profound: **prayer isn't limited to specific times or sacred spaces—it is a way of living, a continual dialogue with God.**

And that brings us to the next part of our journey…

Section 5

Prayer as a Way of Life

Living in Constant Communion with God.

20

Living a Life of Prayer—Turning Every Moment into a Sacred Conversation

Transforming daily routines into moments of worship.

What if prayer wasn't just something you did in the morning or before bed? What if prayer became a constant, natural part of your day—as natural as breathing?

That's exactly what God invites us into:
"Pray without ceasing." — 1 Thessalonians 5:17

At first, that sounds impossible. How can we pray all the time when we have jobs, responsibilities, and busy schedules?

The answer is simple: **We turn every moment into a sacred conversation.** Prayer isn't just about setting aside time—it's about including God in everything.

Jesus' Example: A Life of Constant Prayer

Jesus didn't just pray at designated times—He prayed throughout His day:

✔ He prayed before meals. (*Luke 22:19*)
✔ He prayed before decisions. (*Luke 6:12–13*)
✔ He prayed before miracles. (*John 11:41–42*)
✔ He prayed in gratitude. (*Matthew 11:25*)
✔ He prayed while walking. (*Mark 6:46–48*)
✔ He prayed in pain. (*Matthew 26:39*)

Jesus didn't compartmentalize prayer—it was **woven into everything He did**. And that's how we're meant to live too.

How to Make Everyday Moments Sacred

You don't have to stop what you're doing to pray—you just have to **invite God into it**.

1. **Pray While You Wake Up**
   Before checking your phone, say:
   "Lord, thank You for this new day. Walk with me today."

2. **Pray While You Work**
   As you start your tasks, whisper:
   "God, give me wisdom. Help me work with excellence."

3. **Pray While You Drive**
   Instead of stressing about traffic, say:
   "God, thank You for this moment of stillness. Be with me today."

4. **Pray While You Do Chores**
   Turn ordinary tasks into worship by saying:
   "Lord, I offer this moment to You. Let everything, I do be for Your glory."

5. **Pray When You Feel Overwhelmed**
   Instead of letting anxiety take over, breathe and say:
   "Jesus, I trust You. Give me peace."

6. **Pray Before Bed**
   As you lay down, reflect and say:
   "God, thank You for this day. I rest in Your hands."

The goal is not to force prayer into your schedule—it's to **invite God into everything**.

Why Living a Life of Prayer Changes Everything

✔ It keeps us connected to God throughout the day.
✔ It turns ordinary moments into acts of worship.
✔ It replaces stress with peace.
✔ It deepens our faith in small, daily ways.

Prayer is no longer a task—it becomes **a way of life**.

Guided Prayer: Inviting God into Every Moment

"Father, I don't want prayer to be just something I do—I want it to be part of who I am. Help me to walk with You, talk with You, and invite You into every moment of my day. Let my life be a constant conversation with You. Amen."

Reflection Question

➡ What is one daily routine where you can invite God into the moment?

Testimony: How One Simple Shift Changed My Prayer Life

Marcus used to struggle with staying connected to God. "I would pray in the morning and at night, but during the day, I felt disconnected."

Then he learned about practicing God's presence—**turning every moment into a conversation with God.**

"I started praying while driving, while working, even while making coffee. Instead of making prayer a separate part of my day, I made it part of everything I do."

Now, Marcus doesn't just pray at specific times—**he walks with God all day.**

"Prayer has become a constant rhythm in my life. And the more I talk to God, the more I sense His presence."

That's the secret. **The more you pray, the more aware you become of God in every moment.**

21

A Prayer Life That Lasts—Making Prayer a Daily Habit

Practical ways to make prayer a lifestyle, not an obligation.

Many people start strong in their prayer life—only to lose momentum.
They pray when they're inspired. They pray when they need something. But after a while, life gets busy, and prayer becomes an afterthought.

Sound familiar?

The key to a powerful, lasting prayer life isn't about emotion or waiting for the "right moment." It's about **building daily habits** that keep us connected to God—no matter what.
Jesus had this kind of prayer life. And He invites us to do the same.

Jesus' Example: Consistency in Prayer

Jesus didn't just pray when He felt like it. He had a **regular rhythm of prayer**:

✔ He prayed early in the morning. (*Mark 1:35*)
✔ He prayed before big decisions. (*Luke 6:12*)
✔ He prayed in difficult moments. (*Matthew 26:39*)
✔ He prayed on ordinary days. (*Luke 5:16*)

Prayer wasn't something He added to His life—it was part of His **daily routine**.
If Jesus, the Son of God, needed consistent prayer, how much more do we?

Why Do People Struggle to Pray Consistently?

1. **Busyness**
   "I don't have time to pray."
   But the truth is: **We make time for what matters.**

2. **Distractions**
   Phones, social media, and responsibilities pull us away.
   Solution: Create intentional space for prayer.

3. **Feeling Spiritually Dry**
   "I don't feel anything when I pray."
   Prayer isn't about feelings—it's about **faithfulness**.

4. **Not Knowing What to Say**
   "I run out of things to pray about."
   That's why Jesus gave us models like **The Lord's Prayer!**

How to Make Prayer a Daily Habit

1. **Pick a Time**
   Choose a set time for prayer each day. Morning, lunch, or night—just commit to it.

2. **Create a Prayer Space**
   Find a quiet place where you won't be easily distracted.

3. **Use a Prayer Guide**
   Follow **The Lord's Prayer (Matthew 6:9–13)**, a prayer journal, or Scripture-based prayers.

4. **Pray Throughout the Day**
   Don't limit prayer to just one moment—talk to God all day.

5. **Stay Accountable**
   Find a prayer partner to check in with or use reminders to stay consistent.

Guided Prayer: Asking God for a Consistent Prayer Life

"Father, I want a stronger prayer life. Help me to make prayer a daily habit, not just something I do when I need help. Give me discipline to seek You every day. Let prayer become a natural part of my life. In Jesus' name, Amen."

Reflection Question

➡ What's one small step you can take today to make prayer a daily habit?

Testimony: How Daily Prayer Transformed My Life

For years, Bryan struggled with spiritual inconsistency.
"I would pray here and there, but I wasn't consistent. I let busyness take over."

Then he made one small change—he set an alarm every morning at 6 AM to spend time with God.

"At first, it felt forced. But after a while, I started looking forward to that time."

Over time, his relationship with God deepened, his stress levels dropped, and he found himself praying throughout the day—without even thinking about it.

"Now, I can't imagine a day without prayer. It's not just a habit—it's my lifeline."

22

Living a Life of Love—How Prayer Transforms Who We Are

Letting prayer shape our identity and reflect Christ in our lives.

Prayer is not just about changing our circumstances—it's about changing **us**.

When we spend time with God in prayer, something incredible happens:

✔ Our hearts soften.
✔ Our attitudes shift.
✔ Our actions begin to reflect His love.

Prayer isn't just a tool to ask for things—it's a process that **shapes us into the people God created us to be**.

Jesus' Example: Prayer & Love Are Connected

Jesus was the most loving person to ever walk the earth—and His love was **fueled by prayer**.

✔ He prayed for His enemies. (*Luke 23:34*)
✔ He prayed for His followers. (*John 17:9*)
✔ He prayed for all future believers—including us. (*John 17:20–21*)

Even in His final moments on the cross, Jesus was praying: "Father, forgive them, for they do not know what they are doing." — *Luke 23:34*

How Prayer Transforms Us

1. Prayer Helps Us Love Difficult People.
It's hard to stay bitter toward someone when you pray for them. "Love your enemies and pray for those who persecute you." (*Matthew 5:44*)

2. Prayer Helps Us Become More Like Jesus.
The more time we spend with God, the more we reflect His love, patience, and kindness.
"And we all... are being transformed into His image." (*2 Corinthians 3:18*)

3. Prayer Softens Our Hearts.
Prayer keeps our hearts from becoming cold, hardened, or self-centered.
"Create in me a pure heart, O God." (*Psalm 51:10*)

How to Pray for a More Loving Heart

Who are we? Why were we created? Why are we here? What is our purpose in this life?
Are we here to just take everything we can from others and from the Earth's resources? Or should we **give back—to people and to the planet**?

Will we be tested on how much we obtained and achieved—or on how much we **loved**?

Our fundamental purpose on Earth may be this: **to love and be loved**.

If you want God's love to shine through your life, start with these prayers:

1. **Pray for God to change your heart.**
   "Father, make me more like You. Help me love others the way You do."

2. **Pray for people you struggle to love.**
   "Lord, help me to see this person the way You see them."

3. **Pray for God to give you opportunities to show love.**
   "Father, use me to encourage, serve, and bless others today."

Guided Prayer: Asking God to Transform Your Heart

"Father, I don't want to just pray—I want to be changed. Help me to love all humans as You do. Soften my heart. Fill me with Your love. Help me to forgive, to serve, and to reflect Your kindness in everything I do. Make me more like You. Amen."

Reflection Question

➡ How has prayer changed your heart? Are there people in your life you need to pray for today?

Testimony: How Prayer Helped Me Forgive

Lena had been holding onto bitterness for years. A close friend had betrayed her, and no matter how much time passed, she couldn't let it go.

"Every time I thought about them; I felt anger rise up."

One day, she heard a sermon about praying for your enemies. She resisted at first, but finally, she prayed: "God, I don't want to forgive them. But I know You call me to. Help me let go of this bitterness."

She kept praying. Day after day. And slowly, something shifted.

"It didn't happen overnight. But one day, I realized—I wasn't angry anymore. I was free."

Forgiveness didn't just release the other person—it **released her**. Prayer didn't just change the situation—it **changed her heart**.

23

The Secret to a Powerful Prayer Life—Never Stop Praying

Living a life of continual communion with God.

If there's one thing Jesus modeled in His life, it's this: Prayer isn't just something we do—it's how we live. It's not a once-in-a-while activity or something we turn to only in hard times. It's meant to be a continuous, ongoing, never-ending conversation with God.

That's why Paul tells us: **"Pray without ceasing."** — 1 Thessalonians 5:17

But what does that actually look like? How do we make prayer a lifestyle, not just a habit?

Jesus' Example: A Life of Constant Prayer

Jesus didn't just pray in the morning or at mealtimes—He prayed all the time.

✔ He prayed before decisions. *(Luke 6:12–13)*
✔ He prayed while walking. *(Mark 6:46–48)*
✔ He prayed before miracles. *(John 11:41–42)*
✔ He prayed in His final breath. *(Luke 23:46)*

Prayer wasn't an event in Jesus' day—it was woven into everything He did.

How to "Pray Without Ceasing"

If you want to keep prayer alive in your daily life, start here:

1. **Start Your Day with Prayer**
   Before checking your phone or getting out of bed, say: *"God, I give You this day. Guide me, speak to me, and help me stay close to You."*

2. **Turn Worries into Prayers**
Instead of stressing, say:
"Lord, I give this to You. Help me trust You with it."

3. **Pray Short Prayers Throughout the Day**
You don't have to stop everything to pray. Whisper prayers like:
"Thank You, God, for this moment."
"Help me love this person well."
"Give me wisdom in this situation."

4. **End Your Day in Prayer**
Reflect on the day and say:
"God, thank You for today. Forgive where I fell short. Help me rest in You."

Guided Prayer: Asking God for a Life of Prayer

"Father, I don't want prayer to be something I check off a list. I want it to be part of who I am. Help me to walk with You daily, to talk with You constantly, and to live in Your presence. Teach me to pray without ceasing. Amen."

Reflection Question

➡ What is one way you can weave prayer into your daily routine?

Testimony: How a Simple Shift Transformed My Prayer Life

James always struggled with consistency in prayer. "I thought prayer had to be long, structured, and formal. Because I didn't have time for that, I ended up not praying much at all."

Then he learned about short, constant prayers—inviting God into every moment. "I started praying while driving, while cooking, while working. Just small prayers—'Thank You, God' or 'Lord, help me today.'"

Over time, his entire perspective changed. "Prayer stopped feeling like something I had to schedule. It became part of my daily life. I started sensing God's presence more, because I was talking to Him more."

That's the secret. **The more we pray, the more we experience God.**

Final Words: This Is Just the Beginning

A life of prayer isn't about getting it perfect—it's about staying connected to God. You don't have to pray like anyone else. You don't have to have all the right words. You just have to show up —every day, in every moment—and talk to the One who loves you most.

If you do that, prayer won't just be a practice. It will become the heartbeat of your life. It will become the sacred rhythm that carries you through joy, grief, uncertainty, and peace. It's not about eloquence—it's about honesty. It's not about length—it's about love.

As I shared in the preface, I never intended to write a book on prayer. I simply set out to fulfill a Lenten commitment. But God had other plans—and in saying yes to Him, I discovered something far deeper: that prayer is the gateway to a transformed life. A surrendered life. A joyful life.

I invite you to make the same discovery. Don't just learn about prayer—live it. Let your conversations with God shape your character. Let your time with Him soften your heart. Let your prayers be not a task but a lifeline.

So, if you've ever felt like prayer is out of reach, too complicated, or something only spiritual experts do—hear this: You belong in this conversation. Your voice matters. And your heavenly Father is always listening.

Conclusion: Your Journey Starts Now

This book was never meant to be just something you read—it's something you live. It's a companion, a guide, and a heartfelt invitation into a deeper relationship with the God who created you, knows you, and loves you more than you can imagine.

If you apply what you've learned:

✔ Your faith will grow.
✔ Your heart will change.
✔ Your connection with God will deepen.
✔ Your life will reflect His love in new and beautiful ways.

So don't stop here. Keep praying. Keep listening. Keep surrendering. Keep walking with God.

Because a powerful prayer life isn't built in a day—it's built day by day, moment by moment, one conversation with God at a time.

You don't have to wait for the perfect moment. You don't have to have the right words. You just have to start.

If you remember nothing else from this book, remember this: **Prayer is not about performance—it's about presence.** And presence leads to transformation.

Let God take the lead in your life. Trust Him in the highs and lows, in the silence and the storms. Just as I learned in the cockpit of my own life—when I let go, God took over. And He did more than I could ever ask, think, or imagine.

Now it's your turn.

The journey of prayer doesn't end on the last page of this book —it begins right now, with your next prayer.

So, take a deep breath. Open your heart. And speak to God.

This is your moment. This is your invitation. This is your praying life.

Thank you for reading my words.

ACKNOWLEDGEMNTS

I would like to thank Nour E. Noureddine for her exceptional work in producing the book cover. I'm also deeply grateful to NOT-Y for their contribution to the development, structure, editing, formatting, and overall concept of this book.

I thank God for inspiring me to use my gifts to write a book on prayer—with the hope that it encourages, uplifts, and transforms lives.

To my loving wife—thank you for walking beside me with faith and grace. And to my sons, who inspire me every day: I pray that all good things will come to you in this life, and even more so in the life to come.

BIBLIOGRAPHY

The Holy Bible, English Standard Version. Wheaton, IL: Crossway Bibles, 2001.

The Holy Bible, King James Version. New York: American Bible Society, 1999.

The Holy Bible, New International Version. Colorado Springs, CO: Biblica, 2011.

The Holy Bible, New Revised Standard Version. Division of Christian Education of the National Council of the Churches of Christ in the United States of America, 1989.

The Holy Bible, New Living Translation. Carol Stream, IL: Tyndale House Publishers, 2015.

The Holy Bible, New American Standard Bible. La Habra, CA: The Lockman Foundation, 1995.

Note: Scripture verses have been paraphrased or adapted for clarity, devotional reflection, and readability. Readers are encouraged to explore these passages in their preferred Bible translation for deeper study.

ABOUT THE AUTHOR

Frank J. Donohue, born in New York, is an American pilot, author, publisher and video producer. He earned his bachelor's degree and several pilot licenses at Embry-Riddle Aeronautical University after serving one tour of duty in the United States Air Force. Frank holds the Airline Transport Pilot license, Flight Instructor license, Advanced and Instrument Ground Instructor licenses, Flight Engineer License, Aircraft Dispatcher license and Remote Pilot Certificate. With over 36 years of flying experience, Frank received a prestigious pilot award for over 30 years of impeccable service for a very distinguished career of flying excellence with FedEx in 2018.

Frank is the author of *School and Schooled*, #1 Bestselling author of *Ten Healthy Tips*, author of *From Hate to Love*, author of #1 Bestselling *Frank the Pilot*, author of *God Said to me*, and author of *The Power of a Praying Life*. Frank lives in Virginia Beach with his wife. They have two grown children. He enjoys traveling, gardening, fishing and helping people through various philanthropic organizations.

AUTHOR'S NOTES

The Power of a Praying Life was written, designed, produced and published by its author to the same high standards as the mainstream publishing industry. It is really hard to put a good book together. I invite you to post an honest and objective review of this book in the online bookstore of your choice. Your comments will help improve the quality of what good writers write and what good readers read. Search "books by Frank J. Donohue" to find my books. Thank you for reading my words.

My pilot and love videos are posted on:

TikTok = **NOT_Y4U**
Instagram = **LOVENOTYY4U**
Meta/FB = **NOT-Y** (thru Frank J Donohue)
YouTube = **NOT-Y** (/@not-y2241)
YouTube = **LOVE OF HUMANITY** (/ @Loveofhumanity-vq8go)

End of book